# On
## the Public

With its rich illustrative material and many sharp insights, Hannay's book will both instruct and provoke its readers, challenging those who do not share his diagnosis of the present state of the public sphere to think about why and how it should best be defended.

George Pattison, Christ Church, Oxford

## Praise for the series

'. . . allows a space for distinguished thinkers to write about their passions'

*The Philosophers' Magazine*

'. . . deserve high praise'

Boyd Tonkin, *The Independent* (UK)

'This is clearly an important series. I look forward to reading future volumes.'

Frank Kermode, author of *Shakespeare's Language*

'. . . both rigorous and accessible'

*Humanist News*

'. . . the series looks superb'

*Quentin Skinner*

'. . . an excellent and beautiful series'

Ben Rogers, author of *A.J.Ayer: A Life*

'Routledge's Thinking in Action series is the theory junkie's answer to the eminently pocketable Penguin 60s series.'

*Mute Magazine* (UK)

'Routledge's new series, *Thinking in Action*, brings philosophers to our aid . . .'

*The Evening Standard* (UK)

'. . . a welcome new series by Routledge'

*Bulletin of Science, Technology and Society*

ALASTAIR HANNAY

# **On**
the Public

Routledge
Taylor & Francis Group

LONDON AND NEW YORK

First published 2005
by Routledge
2 Park Square, Milton Park, Abingdon, Oxon OX14 4RN

Simultaneously published in the USA and Canada
by Routledge
270 Madison Ave, New York, NY 10016

*Routledge is an imprint of the Taylor & Francis Group*

Typeset in Joanna MT and DIN by
RefineCatch Ltd, Bungay, Suffolk
Printed and bound in Great Britain by
TJ International Ltd, Padstow, Cornwall

*British Library Cataloguing in Publication Data*
A catalogue record for this book is available from the British Library

*Library of Congress Cataloging in Publication Data*
Hannay, Alastair.
   On the public / Alastair Hannay.-- 1st ed.
      p. cm. -- (Thinking in action)
   Includes bibliographical references.
   ISBN 0–415–32792–X (hardcover : alk. paper) -- ISBN 0–415–32793–8 (pbk. : alk.
paper)   1. Political participation.   2. Democracy.   I. Title.   II. Series.
   JF799.H36 2005
   306.2--dc22                                                    2004015990

ISBN 0–415–32792–X (hbk)
ISBN 0–415–32793–8 (pbk)

This is Brit's book

# Preface

I have to admit that the topic of this book is one that only began to interest me recently. That was during a month-long visit to the USA at the time of the President's decision to go to war in Iraq. I was told on television that he was 'comfortable' with that momentous decision. So, it seems, were most Americans, on and off television. Pick-up trucks boasted the Stars and Stripes, 'God Bless America' was everywhere, and you could almost see the flag in some television journalists' eyes. But many Americans were not comfortable. These included low-income homesteaders, who displayed banners saying money should be spent not on war but on want. Most of my colleagues were against. Some of them confronted a curious dilemma. Those with plans to spend the summer vacation in France risked reprisals, even among colleagues; those bent on Italy could stick to their plans with easy minds.

One thought that struck me at the time, too trivial in the light of such events to dwell on for long, but inescapable for the well-brought-up philosopher, was this: if the US public is divided on the invasion of Iraq, how can we still think of it as 'the' US public? Divide a public, as anything else, and you have not one but two. But do we not, even when the US public is divided, still say that what is divided is the US public? This public, like any similar one, somehow survives division, this division and of course a thousand others. We do not have two publics, or a thousand publics. So what is this notion of 'the' public that stands fast though it is divided?

Other more urgent thoughts occurred to me. The way in which the media, especially television, ran up the flag was one of these. When some rusty cans were discovered by the advancing armada, an excited commentator on a well-known television channel exclaimed that now, surely, it would be 'game, set and match!'. That the press was also divided is true, but critics were mainly confined to the printed word and had to wait a long time before television, in its characteristically vivid manner, began to carry evidence that things were not going all that well. Both the power of the media and the ease with which people were influenced by them caused me to ponder for the first time the nature of the democracy that exists in our modern western societies. Is it really good enough for us to think of exporting it?

There are two opposite ways of looking at our modern version of participatory democracy. One way is to see it as the expression of an ideal in which responsibility for generating good in the world is laid on the shoulders of the individual rather than the state. That would provide an ideological basis for the actual nature of a society where privacy is so privileged and protected. The privacy can then be seen as an opportunity for fulfilling human possibilities in the way these have been traditionally regarded, that is to say, as essentially involving the capacity to cooperate and create equitable forms of coexistence.

But there is a more depressing view. It is that any opportunities for fulfilment on this basis are being increasingly forfeited. That (by no means new) thought underlies and motivates this book. The chapters that follow attempt to indicate and explain the way in which things are thus and nudge the reader in a direction that I think might provide us with an opportunity nevertheless to exploit to human advantage the privileging of privacy.

Our topic is the public but its point of view is that of the public as we know it, or think we do, a public in which, for good or ill, the media play a major role. However, to be clear about the present it helps to look into the past. By, as it were, bouncing our topic and its subtopics back from their past, we are able to see them all from a wider and a deeper perspective. The past, after all, is where habits of speech have their origin, and changing circumstances along the way do not always find their expression in current idiom.

Chapter 1 suggests that our public is not quite the 'public' that our ways of talking about ourselves would lead us to assume. Since that is due largely to the way our society has departed from the one in which our inherited notion had its origins, and in order to locate that origin and highlight the features that were incorporated in it, we deepen the focus and go back to ancient Rome to look at a society that had yet to acquire the feature whose presence our ways of talking tend to assume.

How far, and in what way, has our society departed from the one in which the notion of 'the public' first arose? Chapter 2 returns again to the past, first to the virtual past of Shakespearian history and then to the actual past of the eighteenth century, where another notion, that of 'a public', the public as audience, began to gain ground and to be confused with that of 'the public'.

As an illustration of this confusion, we can turn to some current images familiar to us from the media. Media images reach a wide public. That at least is how we often put it, and no one objects if someone says that the outrage felt at the atrocities disclosed in Abu Ghraib prison was 'worldwide'. By 'worldwide' we often just mean 'across national boundaries'. But, of course, with CNN and its colleagues there are no serious limits to the distribution of such images. It seems perfectly in order, then, to speak of CNN's audience as its worldwide public. The distinction made in Chapter 2 helps us, however, to be clear that while the notion of 'the public' is political, that of 'a' public is only incidentally so.

Chapters 3, 4 and 5 look at the present in the light of the past. The ideal of a public sphere, a sphere of open and free discussion, arose in the eighteenth century, in ways that have been well recounted by others. Chapter 3 re-tells the history in short form in order to show how, even within the fledgling public sphere, this other notion, that of 'a' public, had found a secure footing and with it the distinction between speaking authority and listening public. Chapter 4 teases out the notion of public opinion through visits to Hume and Voltaire. With some notions now of the public, of publics, of the public sphere and of public opinion to back it, Chapter 5 takes a direct look at the present; but even here there is a brief allusion to the past. The topic is that of the takeover of public space by privacy, of what that means, and of the implications for participation by the public in political affairs. Chapter 6 follows with some account of the role in this of the media.

The remainder of the book offers suggestions for staying the damaging effects of the circumstances addressed so far. Chapter 7 promotes a form of common sense in the shape of an ability to detect anomalies both in the utterances of people with the power to direct events and in those who willingly follow their lead. Among these latter we, as often as not, find ourselves. Without going into the details here, the suggestion is that there is an alternative to the objectivist proposals typically advanced by philosophers. A case is paraded for an individual's perspective, though not in abstraction but one born of experience.

In writing this book I have drawn on what has been said on these matters from the time of Cicero. So there is nothing new. But I do try to bring together strands that challenge readers to judge, and at more than one level, some not unfamiliar criticisms of western society. My aim, then, is to offer a critical as well as a descriptive account of what the public amounts to today, and to supply enough in the way of suggestions and arguments to engage the critical faculties of readers, whatever their own views, or whatever conclusions they themselves would wish to draw.

# Acknowledgements

This book began life in a comfortable easy chair in the sitting room of a peaceful home loaned by a friend in California. As I began taking notes, I watched US tanks speeding invincibly towards Baghdad, cheered on by patriotic journalists. For the chair, the home and the peace I thank Marianne McDonald, as also for kindly sending me a book that did much to speed me on my own way. Andrew Feenberg I thank for sharing his wide knowledge of communications literature, and some thoughts on pianos, even before I began; Marit Bakke for a valuable tip on literature; and Brit Berggreen for more of the same and for many an idea. I owe to Arne Johan Vetlesen's acute observations on an early draft a sharpened sense that not all will agree with me. To all of these I can express my appreciation without implicating them in anything they might take exception to in the result. Not so with three anonymous reviewers. Their discerning comments have been quite indispensable in producing the final draft. If mistakes and obscurity remain, blame me. I owe to my publisher, Tony Bruce, special thanks for heading me in the required direction and for valuable criticism, advice and support throughout.

# **One**

We hear and read a lot about the public these days. In the media, the public appears as an important player in national and international politics. If not exactly in the front line, the public is nevertheless presented as a force that political decision-makers must reckon with. Putting drastic plans into effect can depend on a wave of its support, while when events take an unpredicted turn, the politicians may find that it has become their scourge. In the wake of the invasion of Iraq, claims that governments had misled the public about the justification for war littered the press. There is a moral dimension too: 'The British public won't forgive such shameless scape-goating', said one newspaper article, referring to the British government's accusation that the BBC had lied when claiming the government had 'sexed up' the information at its disposal to make a more convincing case for war.[1] Yet, when the tumult dies down, the public often shows itself able to forgive. Or should that not be, rather, to forget?

In spite of its place in the press, we may wonder whether the public proves to be anything like a thing or even personage at all, as opposed to the more or less tangible things we call 'public' (affairs, services, officials, spirit, to say nothing of holidays, parks, baths, libraries, schools, and houses)? After all, to the substantive 'public' there is no corresponding singular noun 'private', only an adjectivally private this that and the other. Still, however intangible this public may prove to be, according to our ordinary ways of speaking we may nevertheless side with it, and it with us. We can sometimes dissent from it, but also offend and outrage it. That seems to show there must be something we can identify as its opinion. But what exactly is public opinion? A kind of collective view of things perhaps, the view people at large have concerning issues of common concern? How can or does the public acquire opinions? Where does it meet? Who draws up its agenda? Furthermore, even if on occasion the public may speak with one voice, that is far from being the rule. That public opinion is frequently split suggests we must dig deeper, or perhaps ascend to some higher and more abstract level, to catch sight of what is meant when we refer to the public.

To ask 'what is the public?' sounds as if we were asking for features of some abstract object, or trying to pin down the public on a chart of 'kinds'. The question sounds abstruse and philosophical. A question apparently far easier to answer would be, 'just who are the public?', for then we can point to each other and say, 'you and I are the public' as, for that matter, is anyone. But as we will see, that answer, if true, although scarcely informative enough at first glance for the question to be worth asking, is in fact highly significant. It is also rather complex, but seeing the complexity will put us then in a position to ask that first question in a somewhat different way. We will be able to ask both 'what is the public?' and 'what became of it?'.

That first question, 'what is the public?', at least has the virtue of capturing the idea we have, at least in our own and other western societies, of the public as some kind of thing, if not always a single body then at least a diffuse source of sometimes conflicting views on this and that – views that make the headlines, but which, as we shall discuss, it is not implausible to suggest that the headlines also help to make. For the present, we are looking at something else. That the public figures quite naturally in our thoughts tends to obscure certain truths about the topic and about our society. Although ordinary ways of speaking might suggest otherwise, the fact that you or I are members of the public does not mean that the public as we think and speak of it is to be found just anywhere. Did Roman citizens form a public? Was there ever an Iraqi public? What about present-day China? If the inclination is to answer 'yes' we may ask ourselves whether the use of 'public' in these cases really does have the same flavour, or whether the same associations really come to mind, as when we speak of the British or the American public, of the French, the German, etc. But if we say 'no', can we say with any certainty just what was missing and what changes would be, or in the case of the Romans would have been, required for such states to acquire their public?

Although by no means an abstruse exercise, perhaps the present attempt to throw light on the notion of the public may still be called philosophical. But then that is because any investigation into some not very obvious or indeed normally considered but central fact deserves the name. That the public figures quite naturally in our thoughts of our own society, that it is a kind of public figure, is a fact that conceals many less immediately accessible facts about the society, its distinctiveness, its possibilities and also its alternatives.

The expression 'members of the public', used just now, is a common one, but it is also rather curious. The idea of membership is typically reserved for a form of association to which the public explicitly has no access. The sign 'Members Only', although addressed to the public, to the majority of the public means 'Keep Out'. But what form of association is being appealed to when a television commentator tells us that along with 'sixteen members of the Royal Family', 'a thousand members of the public' attended the commemorative celebrations of the Coronation of Queen Elizabeth II?

Several questions offer themselves to reflection. What form of membership can apply both to the former and to the latter? Can, and on what terms can, the members of each join with those of the other to form a single public on that occasion?

Consider how reflection on this matter might proceed. To begin with, we might think, all that membership of the public means is entitlement to move freely in what is called public space, in this case one of those spaces where members of the public join together in celebration. In others they assemble as an audience; perhaps in the presence of royalty, members of the 'ordinary' public tend to form an audience. In other public spaces, they are merely there. In general, public spaces are where you find the public. The freedom to be there is enjoyed by anyone 'belonging' to it.

Yet what sense of 'belonging' together is there in just being able to run across one another in places 'open to the public'? As a way of belonging, membership brings to mind ties that link a number of people. These may be the kind of internal and contractual bonds shared by members of a club, or a team, or some other form of association such as families, including royal families. They can be blood ties or ties of convention, or they may be rules one subscribes to in return for commitment to some common aim, whether the pursuit of some esoteric interest or an interest pursued in public, for instance competing with peer associations for prizes. The teams formed by football clubs compete under the rules of membership of a more embracing association for prizes such as the League Cup.

It is difficult to uncover any such basis underlying the title 'member of the public'. It is more difficult even than with the notion of 'member of the human race'. There is underlying the latter at least some taxonomical point in marking us off as belonging to one species rather than another. Though the etymology is more complicated,[2] the customary distinction made by 'public' is with 'private', and that is a socio-political and, especially, a juridical distinction. Moreover, even if we talk of the private domain there is nothing called 'the' private of which you or I, or even some non-personal entity, might be listed as a member.

In the case of the purely taxonomical distinction, there can, on occasion, be something stronger and more existential than just the need to mark one species off from another. The prospect of universal extinction, for example. Consider imminent environmental disaster or a predicted collision with an asteroid on course for Earth. We may readily understand how the threat of collective annihilation and the thought of its tragic implications and the need to face up to them can give members of the species a sense of global belonging, a sense of the kind we capture in phrases like 'all in the same boat'. But could there be a parallel scenario, making global membership of the public an equally possible notion? Might we, in certain circumstances, see ourselves as members of a universal public?

Although it may seem easy enough to envisage a universal public, in the sense of a collective to be part of which implies no geographical or national identity (it is indeed one of the goals or implications of political globalization), it is hard to see how being a part of that collective can be described in terms of membership. Some people claim that globalization strengthens rather than weakens national identities, just as it is claimed that a centrally regulated European Union will be able to protect the integrity of its component states. Like Europeans, universal citizens can still think of themselves as members of their nations, as of whatever other associations are available. It does seem more likely, however, that the idea of nation-membership, by becoming increasingly abstract, will tend to merge in importance, as well as have to compete, with other more dominant associative forms. In the context of the nation we are more likely to talk, whether appropriately or not, of being part of its public, which is expressed 'at home' by saying we are (part of) the public.

But of membership of that public? Well, as noted, the expression is one that springs naturally to the lips. In anticipation of, but also by way of introducing a main line of thought in what follows, we can reflect on one kind of situation that brings the expression as it were into its own. If inclusion in the public means, as I suggest there is good reason to think it does, being accorded some entitlement to state protection, then situations in which that entitlement is invoked can very well induce a sense of membership. It is a sense analogous to that in which subscribers to health schemes or rescue services are referred to as members of, say, Blue Cross. Just as illness activates the notion of this membership, so can a dramatic threat to the nation bring the contractual implications of citizenship into play. Even if those party to such an implicit contract have never deliberately entered into such a thing, its virtual existence and what the state, established as it has been to protect its citizens, owes to 'the public' as a whole becomes an issue in time of national crisis. One may catch such contractual overtones in the way US citizens responded to the terrorist attacks of 11 September 2001. The response can be read in other ways too and in less intellectual terms. There are latent ideas of membership in the history and well-disseminated heritage that US citizens are brought up to share, providing a broader background of latent membership ties that invoke shared nationhood on the analogy of the close ties of family rather than underwritten agreement. Either way, we can get a sense of what it is to feel that one is a member of a public, of a particular public.

Much of what I shall say about the public in this book is negative. But the negativity is of several sorts, not all of it bad. Thus there is no denying that there are many virtues in the fact that there are societies of which it is appropriate to say, as in the case of our own, that people living in them form their public. For reasons that will become clear, it is not appropriate to say that in respect of tribal or theocratic societies, that is, societies whose historical course and whose values are determined by monarchical traditions and stringent religious doctrine. The reasons are those that explain the special nature of what it is for us to be or form a 'public', however that term may be used in other contexts. Nor does the notion of the public properly apply in a police state, whether secular or theocratic. The point, crucially, is that a public in the sense in question must somehow be made up of individuals properly called 'private', and that assumes that they are not under military law or a tyranny. One may, under such conditions, still speak in a derivative way of the public; for instance, of a public kept under a tyrant's thumb. But in that case it is not a functioning public, the 'membership' is not, or is no longer, active. On the other hand, and tellingly in respect of what has just been said about this notion of membership, it is under just such conditions that a sense of actual membership, of sharing something in common, comes to the fore.

As for the negative things I shall say about the public, they are not attempts to defend tyranny or reinstate theocracy. They are directed at the idea itself and what is to be regarded as its highly significant lack of content. They are also directed, later in the discussion, at the damaging effect the notion has when made the cornerstone of political life. It is damaging because, as many writers have pointed out, the public is largely a myth. That myth is still with us and has now begun to appear in the guise of a global public. One conclusion I shall draw from the anomalous nature of the notion of membership of the public is that the less we have reason to talk of a global public, the better. Briefly, for the conditions to become global under which there is a single public, certain wide-ranging changes in the social and cultural ordering of human life would have to be in place. These could be disastrous. From the human point of view it might mean the extinction of the humanity of the human race.

But let us approach this apocalyptic conclusion carefully. First, we need to become clear about how the word 'public' has been and is used. It was in currency long before the liberal politics that made such expressions as 'public opinion' and more lately 'the public sphere' current. This may make us sceptical about what was just claimed, that the notion of *the* public belongs to secular societies, or modern societies, societies run on principles first promulgated in the Age of Enlightenment. Has what is called 'the public' changed all that much in the course of history? And surely we ourselves use the term in a far wider way than this arbitrary confinement of it to modern secular societies suggests. Doesn't history itself tell us the notion is not confined to modern conditions?

Regarding the confinement of the notion to modern society, that has something to do with how this notion is connected to two others: that of the public sphere just mentioned, a social space in which views can be publicly aired and matters of public concern openly discussed and debated, and that of a public opinion, as a voice made audible in that space.

As for what history can tell us about all three notions, we may begin by looking at history itself. Well, not directly. The example is historical but we know it best in Shakespeare's fictional version in *Julius Caesar*. Mark Antony speaks in the market-place to what are referred to in the play as 'citizens'. He does so just after Caesar is assassinated by the conspirators.

According to Shakespeare's source, the Greek biographer and philosopher Plutarch, Mark Antony was giving the 'customary' funeral oration. The custom was that such orations be given in the market-place. Naturally, since that is where 'the people' were. Plutarch continues:

> . . . perceiving the people to be infinitely affected with what he had said, he began to mingle with his praises language of commiseration, and horror at what had happened, and, as he was ending his speech, he took the under-clothes of the dead, and held them up, showing them stains of blood and the holes of the many stabs, calling those that had done this act villains and bloody murderers.

'The people', says Plutarch, were 'excited . . . to such indignation, that they would not defer the funeral, but, making a pile of tables and forms in the very market-place, set fire to it; and every one, taking a brand, ran to the conspirators' houses, to attack them'.[3]

Might not Plutarch equally have said it was the *public* that was driven to this act of vengeance? Was it not the Roman public that Mark Antony knew he would meet in the forum and that he aroused to action?

With an important proviso, to be followed up in the next chapter, about how in another sense Mark Antony's audience is rightly referred to as a public, it will, I think, become clear that to say either of these things would be incorrect.

Etymology is not always, is indeed perhaps seldom, a safe guide to the meanings of words as currently used. But in the cases of 'people' and 'public' it is illuminating for our own discussion to see how, even if we nowadays tend to use these words interchangeably, any actual convergence of their meanings is really a meeting of ideas from opposite corners of the political landscape.

The Latin word *populus* is closely linked to nationhood. It refers to *a* people, or from within the bounds of a nation, to *the*, or *its*, people. But in Roman times the term acquired chiefly political connotations and the people were often identified as those who actually participated in national assemblies and spoke for the nation. In the Roman constitution, the powers of government were divided between senate, magistrates and 'the people'. Assemblies in which the latter participated were appropriately called 'popular', but participation was at first confined to the nobility (*patricii*), it therefore being the latter – to us it will appear strangely – who were identified as 'the people'. Only when commoners (*plebeii*) came to be included in the assemblies, in the course of what must count as the most democratic legislative arrangements to appear in ancient Rome (somewhere in the fourth century BC), did 'the people' begin to acquire something of the sense of *plebs*, 'the common citizens', and then inevitably in certain contexts, especially of uprising, even of 'the rabble' or 'multitude' (*multitudo*).

Just as much a political term as *populus*, the Latin *publicus* referred to other aspects of Rome's political life. What was public was what was shared and open to view. One thing shared was, naturally enough, an interest in the maintenance of that large protective entity, the state. This was the prime concern of government, in which, as we saw, the people were involved to various degrees and in various guises. Derived from this is our notion of 'public affairs', or *res publica*, which, construed in the singular as in Cicero's dialogue *De re publica*, was used to refer to the state, or commonwealth, in general. In Latin the term *res* included the sense of 'property', so that *res publica* would have the sense of things that everyone had some investment in and some power over. The idea of the state, not just as a body politic, but also, or perhaps rather included in it, as a shared property in which all have an interest and also an ear, if not always a voice, is just what our own concept of a commonwealth is intended to capture. In Roman times possession and use of *res* in general was part of the people's freedom and a source of civic satisfaction, while loss of it in times of dictatorship could lead to a revolt of the masses and their seizure of power. In Cicero's dialogue a nation run in the name of the people would no longer be a *res publica* but a *res populi*.[4]

Not all debate on public affairs was itself public in the sense of being open to view. The senate's meetings were closed. Nor were popular assemblies necessarily public in the way that, say, senatorial hearings in the United States are today, or sittings of the House of Commons. 'Public' in this sense would refer to those events, political or otherwise, to which the people had access as spectators. Whatever debates, trials, to say nothing of spectacles and 'circuses' of the kind presented at the Colosseum, were public in this restricted auditor's sense, there is no basis here for saying that those who witnessed these were members of the public. The Roman experience gives us no sense yet of what such a public, as opposed to the 'people' in a sense similar to that of the 'commons' (who were indeed represented), might be to whom or to which these proceedings could be open. Least of all does it give us a sense of how the public, again as opposed to the people, might take an active part in political affairs.

That Mark Antony spoke in the market-place was no coincidence. In Rome, as also in ancient Greece, the forum (or agora respectively) was originally just a market-place (at least in so far as any market-place can be just that), only later becoming a centre of civic activity. This was the natural venue for the greatest gatherings, and business transactions would take place there as a matter of course. It was a place where people could exchange gossip and views as well as goods, and flock to hear the latest rumours. They could catch sight of those who decided the course of political events. Not least the latter could make themselves visible there and get some sense of the strength of support for their projects or of the different factions among the people. In some obvious senses, as well as in some less obvious, the Roman forum was thus a public space. And the political role played by those who gathered there, outside the senate, the courts and assemblies, was vital in many ways, even if it was only a supporting one. The people's support was important enough, since its weight in sheer numbers was needed for the carrying out of policies.

That was particularly true at the time of the events Plutarch recounts. Up to then 'the voice of the people' (*vox populi*) only counted when it spoke in the name of the popular assemblies, however these were constituted. But as Mark Antony addressed his audience, the democratic advances previously made in Roman society had largely been reversed by the very man whose death occasioned the speech. Now, more than previously, it was only in the forum that the voice of the people could make itself heard, and if once made up only of patricians, the people were now the populace. From the point of view of the current patricians, however, listening to that voice was necessary if they were to know which way the wind was blowing, if only to be ready to make it blow in another direction, should that be necessary. Disaffection, if wide-spread, would be a hindrance to the recruitment of willing armies and to effecting political change at home. Shakespeare has Mark Antony beg those assembled to lend him their ears.[5] Not, be it noted, as free individuals with protected areas of privacy before whom he, former tribune of the plebs, now triumvir (custodian of the public peace), and would-be successor to Julius Caesar, must put his own case, but so that by bending their minds he could seek support for the succes-sion. Thus it was that once he sensed the effect his words had already made upon those assembled, Mark Antony seized the opportunity and (through, in Shakespeare's rendition, a superb piece of crowd manipulation) turned them into incendiarists.

As we noted, Shakespeare identifies the members of the audience as citizens. Rightly. The civil status of *Civis Romanus* had been instituted as a title with rights attached. In the time of the republic it applied to all free inhabitants of Italy but was later extended to all members of the Roman Empire. The title had a powerful symbolic value that brought peoples with different backgrounds into a far-flung fellowship. Its embody-ing actual rights that protected the individual certainly helped in this respect, for instance the right not to be interrogated by torture.[6] Citizens also possessed the vote but, importantly, it could only be cast in Rome, while those between seventeen and sixty were always liable to military service, usually well away from the capital. In a world lacking our modern means of communication, citizenship therefore meant very little politically. What it did was provide members of an extensive empire with a strong sense of superiority through shared membership of something of supreme value, just as soldiers are inspired to loyalty through indoctrination into a cele-brated (often noisily as well as visibly) heroic tradition. If the historical Marcus Antonius addressed his audience in any-thing like the conciliatory manner of Shakespeare's version, that audience need have detected nothing patronizing or manipulative in 'Friends, Romans, countrymen'. They would appreciate the directness and Mark Antony could count on the sense of a shared destiny behind this appreciation. It was a given that his rhetoric could exploit.

Suppose we now move forward in time to the Roman forum of today. There it is, full of tourists, some in groups together with their guides, and ice-water sellers, all mingling in the ruins of the market-place, the very place where, going on 2000 years ago, Mark Antony addressed his fellow Romans. There is a bomb scare and the *carabinieri* arrive in force to clear the area. A stentorian voice comes over the bull horn, 'Will the public please leave as quickly as possible', the same request repeated in several languages. They leave, while various custodians of the peace remain. Why might we feel this form of address appropriate in this situation?

We note first how general it is. It makes no national distinc-tion. By the same token, no account is taken of whatever political identities those addressed possess in their native contexts. If at home they would form part of their nation's public, a public that is of no account in the present context.

These are simply individuals with the economic resources required of people exercising their rights to traverse a foreign piece of public ground. For the tourist, a visit to the forum is just one aspect, a fringe benefit as it were, of being the kind of ubiquitously mobile private citizen that characterizes modern societies. The forum is part of a space within which such infinitely mobile individuals can freely move.

This answer might indicate a simple way of identifying 'members' of the public. We could say that it is simply by virtue of occupancy of this or any other particular public location that such 'membership' is earned. After all, even when we have dispersed, and so long as we do not enter private houses unasked or public offices outside opening hours, or places where 'public' affairs are being conducted in camera, we are still occupying some portion of public space. Why then should not occupancy of any such space be what makes it appropriate to collect us under this general term 'the public'? We cease being identifiable as members of the public once we have returned to our hotel rooms, or more emphatically perhaps when we finally arrive home and close our garden gates or front doors.

But the answer and the identification are defective and also misleading. Though physical public space is where you meet the public and become it, the notion of space that defines the modern public is abstract and more complex than examples such as the forum as a tourist attraction can provide. What that particular example does show is that, in contexts such as this, with an 'invasion' of tourists, the anonymity of the public extends also to national anonymity, thus obscuring the way in which the notion of the public is a political one and tied to 'membership' of some identifiable body politic. But there are other requirements too that need bringing into the open.

We can throw light on them by introducing a general notion of public space in the abstract and more complex sense we need. That will allow us to see how the public's occupancy of such a space differs both from other ways of occupying it and from its time-to-time occupancy of such sheerly physical locations as streets, pedestrian precincts, public gardens, art galleries, sports stadiums and other spaces reserved for 'the public'.

In its more abstract sense the term 'public space' indicates the presence and possession of shared knowledge and interests. Although the interests people share are far from being exclusively political, it is through the idea of the public good served by political and public life that a public space acquires its prime etymological right to the title 'public'. Yes, we can say that soccer fans occupy a public space in something like this sense, as opposed to the stadiums themselves, but in saying it we are merely acknowledging that a large number of people know who is who and what is what in the now-international world of soccer. Basically, there is a public space in the wide, or secondary, sense wherever there is a topic of conversation that can be focused on by several individuals. Normally, the focus will be on something visible or audible or both, the Roman forum or an opera performance for instance, or, for mathematicians and micro-physicists the notions manifested in significant marks on paper or a black-board. Usually, the shared interests forming the public spaces people inhabit lead them to occupy parts of sheerly physical public space too. But even the very occupying of such spaces can be what forms a public space in this other sense. Inhabitants of a city or village or a piece of countryside occupy geographically bounded areas but in doing so they also share public spaces formed by the contents familiar to them: buildings, sights, landscapes, personalities and so on, all of which form backgrounds to their lives. The notion of space here is clearly metaphorical; it is shorthand for a notion that would have to be analysed in terms of a demography of shared beliefs, interests and topics.

But to occupy a public space more properly so-called is to share with others an ability to identify political leaders and public figures; it is to know and relate to those responsible to you as a 'member' of the public whose interests a government claims to serve. It is to know these figures in at least the quasi-personal way that journalism and the media in general make possible nowadays. It is to share much besides, into the bargain; but, increasingly, the other interests people share, interests outside their own political allegiances, are becoming shared across political boundaries. Those they share in their own political situations form a special kind of ambience, a sense of belonging, of sheltering as it were under a common political umbrella. What binds you under its protection, a protection that is as much psychological, because identity-forming, as political, to whatever extent it succeeds in being the latter at all, is a familiarity with the names and reputations of the main players responsible for the social conditions in which you live.

Returning now to those tourists, we can say that in the typical case only a few will share ambiences. Some will even be at a loss, though less surprisingly perhaps than in some other countries, to label the government or name the prime minister of the country they are visiting. Even if the whole world knows of a Berlusconi, it is at least typical of Europeans to know less of the politics of neighbouring and near-neighbouring countries than of that of their own. By contrast, despite the greater size of the USA and its claims, too, to at least as much cultural diversity as Europe, to describe US citizens as inhabitants of a single public space appears more plausible. The forces that keep the American ambience umbrella largely intact are complex, but the existence of a powerful and centralized press corps must be one of these. The ability to present a unified picture of the state of national affairs is a strong tool of government. There are other forces at work too, but we will return to these later.

Our tourists, then, are not 'the public'. We did hint that there is nevertheless a sense in which they are 'a' public. That, too, is something to which we will return. Here we need to recall that the people who flocked to the ancient forum in Rome were not 'the public' either. What then is it we, or any of our tourists, must possess that they lacked to qualify for that label? Just what does it take to inhabit a public space, properly speaking, in a way that allows us to say that in inhabiting it we are 'its public'?

Well, you may ask, didn't the Romans share knowledge and interests in the way we described, the way that defines a public space? Surely they did. They knew their leaders, they had a strong sense of shared identity, and they were listened to; in matters of war and succession it was impossible for the elite to conduct affairs in ways of which the populace did not approve. So why can we not call them the Roman public?

We may think, provisionally, of the presence of a public in the modern sense of the word as requiring the presence of two things absent in ancient societies. We have already hinted at one. Today the good of the community is thought of primarily in terms of the good of its individual members, the private citizenry, and of their descendants; and the individuals themselves must be thought of as each having a say in what that good amounts to, as well as in how to bring it about and how to maintain it. What is meant by that somewhat misleading term 'member of the public' is a matter of a person's being considered a free and rational being. The freedom in question is not just an entitlement to occupy public spaces, or the possibility of sharing a public space, as above, both of which could be enjoyed by the Roman. It includes the freedom to influence public debate. In ancient times this influence depended on the institutions of civic and political life living alongside the people they served, people on whose allegiance and support 'officialdom' to a large degree depended. It was a matter of proximity and chance, there was no political arrangement whereby the individual citizen as such could have a say, and certainly not wherever geographically placed. Very few individual members of the nation or community had an active say in how to deal with public welfare. Those who did spoke as representatives, but not in the sense, our sense, of carrying a mandate from an electorate. These representatives were embodiments of the people, for political purposes they were the people, while for the represented there was no other recourse than to join in the chorus of the *vox populi*. But that chorus had to be coaxed to exist at all: it did not naturally speak with one voice. In sum, in Roman society the collective good was not conceived, as it is in ours, as the sum of the good of all members of the community individually. Consideration of the public good was tied ultimately and directly not to individuals as such but to the nation and its glory and to the state that maintained both. Conversely, the good of the individual was subservient to the glory of the nation and the well-being of the state. The individually courageous and powerful would be seen as personifications of that glory and well-being, just as state spectacles would be the nation or state itself on display, the public performance in some literal sense a performance both by and of the state.

Earlier it was stated that Roman citizenship provided members of an extensive empire with a sense of superiority through shared membership in something of supreme value. The somewhat paradoxical consequence is that there is more reason to describe the Roman citizens' relationship to the state in 'membership' terms than there is in the case of ours to our own. But then there is conversely less reason to describe their membership as being that of the Roman public. Although it conceals another side, namely the rights of individual privacy, the visible hallmark of the public in our own day is anonymity. We may make ourselves known in public, to a public, but when we do that it is to an audience, another kind of public; it is not a matter of one member of the public making itself known to another or to others. The stereotypes of the public today include the rush-hour throng and the Saturday afternoon football crowd. Not even a composition of units or atoms, this public is an amorphous nothing into which individuals merge. It is, of course, easy to imagine groupings of individuals drawn from this public, samples of the public grouped under several headings: patients in a waiting room, travellers at a boarding gate, spectators at a football match. These can be counted, indeed they usually are, but the labels themselves tell us we are no longer talking about the public. We are talking about private citizens going about their several activities. The term 'the public' is not itself a label of that kind. There is no characteristic activity or set of activities that sets you off as an instance of the public. At best these labelled groupings are formed by members of the public, but we have noted the difficulty with this notion of membership. And of course the public itself is not a wider grouping, one that you might imagine being assembled in a vast reservoir from which these other groupings draw.

We can exploit the reservoir analogy. Logicians distinguish a count-noun from a mass-noun. In drawing water for a drink, what you enjoy is a drink of water. You may enjoy several. But water itself is neither one nor two; it is something, the same thing, that you encounter each time you draw water from a tap. When buying a woollen jersey you choose among several, so 'jersey' is a count-noun, but at the same time, in testing its quality, you are in touch with wool as such, as against cotton or acrylic fibre. So too with the public; you need just one sample to have it in view. By arriving at the actual number of societies that have a public, you will of course be able to say there are so many publics, and in this 'public' differs from 'water'. For every one of those societies, however, there is just one and anyone is it.

The point of saying 'the public' in a political context, however, is not to indicate the truism that in each state that has a public there is only one. The distinction is a theoretical or organizational one, within a state, that distinguishes one political category from others. In this perspective it is not at all hard to speak of the public as some quasi-tangible thing, for instance as that body to which political and public life is responsible. Still, it is a strange kind of body. If someone says to you, 'Show me this public of yours', it would be misguided as well as misleading to say, 'I can't, there are just too many to collect in one place'. The impracticability of assembling all those to whom political life in a given state or commonwealth is responsible, so as to catch a panoptic sight of them, is not to the point. Your questioner should be satisfied by your directing his or her attention to the window and pointing to a passer-by. There is nothing more to find out about the public as such than that you tend to meet it in public places or nature reserves and the like. If the time of day and the speed with which passers-by proceed indicate to you that these are not Sunday strollers but commuters on the way to work, then that tells you what these individuals are up to, not what some part of the public is doing.

A person *appears* as a 'member' of the public in the guise not of 'someone' but of 'anyone'. In the modern world it is within the protected boundaries of one's privacy that one can be, or fail to be, in any fundamental sense *someone*. One aspect of the anonymity that overtakes one when identifiable merely as one of the public is the protection it provides to the private citizen. It is a kind of incognito, a burkha behind which the someone one is remains a secret. Considered 'in itself' the public is faceless, amorphous. In its appearances, as we encounter it, the public is a more or less arbitrary, context-dependent sampling of private individuals abstracted from their privacy.

Yet, according to its official origins this is only half of the story. Or rather, it is the outcome of a development that offers materials for a fuller story, that of the public's rise and fall. Historically, rather than as an incognito to hide behind, the public was once a badge which citizens were proud to bear and eager to show. The public formed a recognizable political grouping whose members recognized each other as such over and above their status as private citizens. Indeed the two would be seen to go together. The public originally formed itself in order to create and protect the conditions of private citizenship. The story is a plausible one at least in the case of a settler nation such as the USA, where the emergence of a public able to call itself 'the public' need not be left to the workings and manipulation of forces already in play. The

American philosopher John Dewey proposes a 'generic' hypothesis on the origins of 'the public', that is, for any such public in the American context. The public arose, he claims, in answer to a demand by 'a group distinctive enough to require recognition and a name'. The name they chose was 'the public'.

> This public is organized and made effective by means of representatives who as guardians of custom, as legislators, as executives, judges, etc., care for its especial interests by methods intended to regulate the conjoint actions of individuals and groups. Then and in so far, association adds to itself political organization, and something which may be government comes into being: the public is a political state.[7]

Dewey defines a 'state' as a 'public articulated and operating through representative officers'.[8] The public thus articulated, 'consists of all those who are affected by the indirect consequences of transactions to such an extent that it is deemed necessary to have those consequences systematically cared for'. They are cared for by 'officials' while representatives oversee the interests of those of the public who are not in on any particular transactions. The material property, funds, etc. needed to undertake this protective role 'are *res publica*, the common-wealth', while the public thus organized 'by means of officials and material agencies', says Dewey, 'is the *Populus*'.[9]

In the society in which he himself lived, however, this identity of public and people was no longer a fact, if it ever had been, for Dewey's public was based on the idea of quite small, close-knit communities. He himself says that the practices and ideas employed in the USA are borrowed from England and based on the 'local town-meeting', while 'we live and act and have our being in a continental national state' and the bonds that tie US citizens are 'non-political'.[10] Dewey talks of the 'eclipse' of the public, but in two ways. On the one hand he says it is not the case that there is no public, in the sense of a 'large body of persons having a common interest in the consequences of social transactions'; on the contrary, '[t]here is too much public, a public too diffused and scattered and too intricate in composition'. This presents a picture of a public too thinly spread to gather itself under one organization. But Dewey also has another way of saying this. He says 'there are too many publics',[11] meaning that, in a large and ramified modern state, the general formula for a public can be found to be satisfied by groups within the state, organizing themselves in the way the public, as the populus, should, but by their very doing so undermining the possibility of a public as the populus.

Does this latter threaten the status of our truism, that in each society that has a public there is only one? Not if the fact that there are several really does mean that there is no single public. But even if there were reason to doubt that, the notion of a public employed in this alternative description of the eclipse of the public is clearly metaphorical. Just as in speaking of a state-within-the-state we know we are not talking literally of a state but of a centre of power and interest isolated from influence by (though not always from influence upon) the larger community, so too in talking of publics in the plural we are not suggesting that a single state could comprise two or more publics 'articulated and operating through representative officers'.

To talk of the public as a phantom, or as a myth, or to refer to its eclipse, is not to say there is no public. You may rather put it, in Dewey's first way, by saying there is 'too much' public. By that, however, he means there are too many worlds of interest, too much engagement in a diversity of topics, special worlds, for all these to be brought together into 'an integrated whole'.[12] Here, in this book, another perspective is being offered. The public still exists – yes, very much so, for it is all around us, and we are it. But it is a public that eschews politics and pursues private interests, it is a public in a new context, one in which society no longer supports the conditions under which what once was referred to as 'the public' came into being. So, if 'the public' is an expression we still use in describing our occupancy of the public spaces we inhabit today, then its meaning differs from that of the name chosen for Dewey's 'distinctive grouping'. As for his use of the plural form, in the following chapter we will exploit an alternative model for talking of publics. It has the advantage over Dewey's derivation of the plural form of providing us with an entirely literal use for the expression 'public'. How far this literal use might replace what in Dewey seems clearly to be a metaphor is something that can be left to the reader to judge.

Public as Audience

# Two

For the provenance of this other use of the noun 'public' we must look to the seventeenth and eighteenth centuries. It was a time that saw the birth and rapid growth of an energetic middle class, and with it a spawning of a variety of spheres, or 'worlds', of interest, commercial, cultural or political, or a mixture of these. It is here we find our publics. Rather than trying to grasp them by comparing them with the political public, as though they were satellite states within the state, and each public an encapsulated self-ordering population within the one body politic, we may see them rather as spaces formed within the state by a proliferation of opportunities for improvement and the enhancement of life. However, the appreciation of such opportunities is not always endemic to those who grasp them; interest often, even typically, has to be aroused, and that realization makes us reflect on how interests can be generated and publics created and manipulated. That thought directs our attention further towards authority, its influence and its variety.

Let us start by returning once more to Mark Antony and the Roman forum. There is clearly a sense – and this is the proviso noted at the beginning of the previous chapter – in which Mark Antony's audience in the forum though, as was argued, not the public was nevertheless *a* public. It was *his* public.

In some pedantic sense it would have been that even if his appeal had been greeted by boos and jeering. Just as the ruined forum today, by becoming a focus of attention for tourists, forms the latter in a manner of speaking, and however transiently, into its public, so too simply by lending him their ears, those who were present when Mark Antony held his funeral oration formed his public. But this public became his also in a stronger and more significant sense. If he first caught its ear, for which he only had to raise his voice, what he later held was its mind. Once he 'perceived', as Plutarch has it, that it had become 'infinitely affected with what he had said', this audience was truly 'his'.

Publics in this sense can be thought of as expandable audiences, though the statistics on knowledge, popularity and taste tell us that they also shrink. Take the Adam brothers, the architects Robert and James, who revolutionized their art in the eighteenth century. They transformed the prevailing pseudo-classical Palladian style, named after the Italian architect Andrea Palladio, by developing romantically elegant variations on diverse classical originals. Commenting on their own achievements, they wrote: 'We flatter ourselves we have been able to seize, with some degree of success, the beautiful spirit of antiquity, and to transfuse it, with novelty and variety, through all our numerous works.' As to whether they had succeeded, they would leave that 'to an impartial public'.

As a commentator remarks: 'In so far as that impartial public consisted of wealthy patrons in both England and Scotland, the answer was resoundingly positive.'[1] Narrowly conceived, the Adams' public consisted only of those who both liked what they saw and also could afford to buy it. More widely conceived, however, it consisted and still consists of all those able or prepared to judge what they saw or can still see.

In a still wider context, though more thinly conceived, it has come to include art historians, ordinary onlookers, or for that matter, yes, again, tourists. Anyone passing Home House in London's Portland Square for the first time and glancing at that building with approval, or even just discernment, might be considered a new member of the Adams' public.

The way in which we talk of buildings, books, plays, their architects, authors and playwrights, as well as composers, songwriters and entertainers, having their publics provides a basis for saying that a public can be more than a mere aggregate of individuals. So one line of thought to be developed below, not least when we take up the topic of public opinion, is that the way in which the public shapes an opinion resembles quite closely that in which *aficionados* respond to works of art, or to the work of individual artists, pop groups, or different kinds of music. A corollary can be offered for our present context: if in one sense the public shapes an opinion, in another perhaps not altogether different sense it is the opinion that forms the public. Combining these is the notion of an interest. Since interests are diverse we must now be prepared to talk, as in such a context we do quite naturally, not just of the public but of a multiplicity of publics.[2]

This will prove significant in that the notion of public opinion is commonly thought of as the opinion of a unified public. There is also, once again, the matter of space. With these multiple publics the connection with actual public space becomes merely incidental. If the market interests that secure artists their publics may motivate a visit to the Tate, or to Madison Square Garden, or the local youth centre, they can also bring their clients' products into the home. Coffee tables with their art books and a teenager's den with its CD and DVD collection are just as much a part of this public's space, and by the same token they become even a kind of public space.

Whatever importance this extension of the space occupied by a public may have for our notions of privacy, amongst others, we shall not delay to discuss this in detail. There is, however, one aspect worth noting by way of illustration and which may lead to further reflections on the sense of 'public' here discussed, namely, the effect of technological advances in the amplification and the recording of sound. Before concert grand pianos were made possible by building a horizontal steel frame into a keyboard instrument, the sound that pianists were able to produce carried only to a fairly small group of listeners placed closely round the performer, and typical audiences consisted of some patron's social circle. Before the harp was provided with hammers to form a keyboard instrument, the audience would have been even smaller. But now, with the sound able to reach the far end of a large hall, the privacy of the soirée or palace recital gives way to the public performance in the concert hall. Later developments have made it possible to hear performers in vast arenas, but then equally in the privacy of one's home, a privacy much greater than the one in which the whole development began. Note that in calling the performance now a public one, we are returning to that other sense of 'public' where what is public is something that may be performed in private but can now reach the ears of others than those of an inner circle. The 'public' that expands in this way is of course a public in the present second sense, defined by the focus of a shared interest, but recruited – at least in our society – from among what provisionally we have only been able to define negatively, namely the public.

But is there, in this sense of a public where it is natural to talk of several publics, some implication that the audience is nevertheless only a 'public' properly so called when the transition has been made from a private to an 'open' hearing? Does a jazz singer acquire a public only if those for whom he or she sings have bought tickets that anyone might have purchased? If so, the concept of public as audience is complex. It implicates all three of the principal connotations of 'public': the audience is 'a public' only when formed of persons drawn from 'the public' in performances that are 'in public'. Being drawn from 'the public' is a matter of the accessibility in principle of what is being presented to just anyone, even if in practice it may be only a very small subsection of the public that would dream of buying tickets.[3]

Still, it is interesting to ponder how far this, our second sense of 'public' may nevertheless apply to the interests of coteries whose 'performances' are not public because held in private. For coteries can be large enough to form what we might allow was indeed a public, that is to say an audience large enough to count as 'a public', yet still not have 'the public' as its audience as it would if its offerings had been given 'in public'. This applies, more obviously perhaps, to clubs, some of which are devised simply to distinguish within the public between acceptable and unacceptable guests. If those allowed entry are still 'the public', that would add strength to the assumption that, in respect of whatever entertainments are offered there, they are just 'a public', an audience drawn from 'the public'.

Again, we may wonder whether, where a topic is too specialized to capture wide interest, those who meet to share their engagement in it, even where discussion is officially open to the public, can properly be said to form a public. If not, then in the case of special interests with audiences too small to form their own public it is always possible for them to shelter under the umbrella of a larger, generic interest, such as music or fine art. Devotees of traditional jazz may not be numerous enough to form a public, but to the music industry they are part of a jazz public that includes fans who appreciate styles established later than the 1920s and which the former abhor. Since the term 'public' in this sense is now largely appropriated by market interests indifferent to such internal distinctions and differences, reasons of this kind for denying the existence of publics tend to vanish from view.

There can be other reasons for not wanting to belong to a public, reasons that do not in this way vanish. Following one special connotation of 'public', devotees of literary theory, for instance, might deny that their interest was such as to generate a public, the reason being not lack of numbers but the fact that the topic is too esoteric or requires too much cultivation to appeal to anything so plebeian as a public.

Finally, the technological developments mentioned earlier weaken and even sever the link between two of our senses of 'public': clearly someone who, in the privacy of their home, plays a publicly available video or sound recording is not by virtue of the latter fact hearing a performance 'in' public. But as was suggested, this person is still occupying a kind of public space, an abstract arena as it were, in which interests that are shared are not shared in public, and in an important sense therefore not shared at all, but repeated individually in a multitude of privacies.

Luckily our intuitions or conclusions on these matters are of no great relevance for the discussion that follows. Though bearing the consequences of technology in mind, what we must chiefly keep a firm hold on is the 'logic' that, in their origins, holds the three main uses of 'public' together.

There is, however, another factor to note. In many areas of shared interests, and perhaps in coteries in general, the notion of a public in the sense discussed in this chapter can become otiose. That is so where the sharing takes the form of performers appreciating each others' performances. Being able to form a public is not merely a matter of numbers, there is also a distance to account for: the distance between performer and audience. What is called audience participation may seem to belie this, but typically it does not. On the contrary, audiences invited to participate in a performance are nothing like the performers themselves, part of whose performance is to co-opt members of the audience and get them to do what they, the performers, want.

That is a possible analogy worth remembering. How far it extends to the contemporary political situation in states that have their (unique) publics is a matter of debate and judgement. But the degree to which supposedly unique publics in that sense have become multiple audiences as described here is a question as crucial as it is topical. Dewey's paradigmatic public is by no means an audience. It is a sufficiently but not too large group of people with a shared interest in the regulation of the consequences of their joint actions, self-positioned in a political system of which they are consciously at one and the same time the private originators and common beneficiaries. The state that does the regulating is the outcome of the wishes of those who in the first instance form it and in later instances support it. If 'the' public becomes no more than an assemblage of unintegrated publics-as-audiences, so that society is split into established executive authority on the one side and interested spectators on the other, there is little to be said for 'the public' in terms of that expression's origin.

The Public Sphere
# Three

The public as audience is remarked on by Jürgen Habermas in his classic study, *The Structural Transformation of the Public Sphere*. He observes that in 'seventeenth-century France *le public* meant the *lecteurs, spectateurs,* and *auditeurs* as the addressees and consumers, and the critics of art and literature . . .'.[1] This is exactly the notion discussed in the previous chapter. Publics form themselves around visible and audible focuses of attention, whether these are particular objects, persons, projects or political programmes – topics, in other words, that groups with a certain background find worth looking at, listening to and at times even, where appropriate, find themselves stimulated to act upon. The background is important in two ways: on the one hand critical audiences are formed by those *select* parts of the populace with the education and resources required to appreciate and consume cultural artefacts, while on the other, where the topics are of public concern, many more than those with that background may be stimulated to action.

So what is this public sphere? Let us start with a simple story sketchily told that at least heads us in the right direction. The details may then be seen the more readily to fall in place. Here is the simple story: a burgeoning middle class, with its diverse interests, quickly finds itself constrained by extant political arrangements, constrained culturally, commercially, and not least, and from a practical point of view first and foremost, politically. That constraint motivates much of its creative spirit, so that the literature it produces is for obvious reasons directed in various ways at the political situation. Talented authors and commentators gain their audiences and engender debate. A discussion on how to run things is carried on, at first in these limited circles but then later, as democratic procedures begin to gain a footing, the discussion is widened, very much so when the press becomes involved. The place where the discussion occurs, an abstract space collecting all the venues, is what is called the public sphere.

The public sphere can exist before the public as such exists. As we said earlier, in order for a state to have its public there must be a system of government designed to protect the rights of individual citizens. However, before that system is in place, so long as it is possible for some people in the society in question freely and openly to discuss the prospects of everyone taking part, equally freely and openly, in such discussion, the public sphere has at least a fledgling existence. The idea of a public sphere is therefore in a sense normative; even in its fledgling beginning where few take part, the idea it represents is one of universal access. That idea was its *raison d'être*. 'The public sphere of civil society', as Habermas himself points out, 'stood or fell with [this] principle', so that '[a] public sphere from which specific groups would *eo ipso* be excluded was less than merely incomplete, it was not a public sphere at all'.[2]

However, we shall see that the notion of 'public' here is, as always, complex. The sphere we call public is in one sense a kind of abstract commons, an area of public space (Habermas's word is 'Öffentlichkeit' – openness or publicity), a room for manoeuvre that had to be created in defiance of the interests and de facto private confines of an absolute power. But the public sphere is also an arena in which matters are conducted 'in public'.

Habermas's discussion of this open space traces it back to the European and British Enlightenment and its emergence in the change from political absolutism to a bourgeois society. Although the focus in discussions of the public sphere is usually on political debate it would however be misleading to suggest this was the only or even the main interest manifested in the emergence of an arena where effective discussion could be joined by people outside the confines of an absolute authority. The public sphere is a space, a kind of noticeboard, one might say, on which private citizens can publish not just their political views but the products of their science and of their art. In making his discoveries known to the world after years of seclusion working up his theories,[3] Isaac Newton was contributing, if you like, to the furnishing of this open space. The metaphor has its limitations. He was not, of course, cluttering the space with furniture in a way that left less room; on the contrary he was enlarging the space by providing it with something new for examination and discussion by others than those with unaccountable authority. That there is a form of cluttering too is a matter we will return to, but the crux itself, regarding the public sphere, is the transition whereby debate on any subject becomes public. What had been private and became public were areas of learning and expertise, and also, be it noted, of authority. Once made open, authority too could be questioned and discussed by those qualified to do so, not now by position but by critical ability.

As is now widely accepted, not least due to Habermas, the public sphere arose when writers and intellectuals, their discussions hitherto confined to the privacy of salons, began to occupy premises on the street. The 'street' factor introduces another aspect of publicness. Although not just anyone could drop in to the coffee-house, it required no invitation to do so. Naturally, to be able to discuss the latest literature one had to be both literate and educated, and to be heard among the experts forming the core of literary discussion required some force of opinion and personality. That of course was no doubt true also in the salons, and it would be wrong to minimize the role these played in the forming of a public sphere. Were some enlightened hostess to invite members of different stations and estates to her soirées, on the basis of their interest and not of their wealth or position, or were she to advertise her soirées in ways available to a wider audience, she would in effect have been taking a first step in the direction of transforming her home into an actual part of that sphere.

But the word 'public' applies here in yet another way. One important function of the salon was to break down social barriers through their very composition, though in varying degrees. The most celebrated salon was that of Mme Germaine de Staël. It was held in Switzerland, by Lake Geneva, where in 1803 she had moved after Napoleon banished her from France for her progressive political views and, not least, her outspoken praise of Germany. The publicity attracted by 'The Salon of Europe', as it was dubbed, centred as much if not more on the famous names collected there as on the views exchanged or passed on. Its gatherings of distinguished intellectuals, writers and aristocrats included musical entertainment, plays and poetry readings. However, another salon was provided in Germany itself, in a far less palatial setting, in the years from 1790 to 1806. Rahel Varnhagen (née Levin) was the enterprising daughter of a Jewish father who had been fortunate, at a time when Jews were under heavy restrictions, including only being allowed to use only two of the many gates into Berlin, to receive a licence to establish himself in business in that city. Without inheritance after her father died, and unmarried for some time to come, the nineteen-year-old Rahel opened a salon that brought together under the same attic roof not only both Jews and Christians but also poor writers who mingled with the most eminent literary figures of the time: Friedrich Schlegel, the Humboldt brothers, Friedrich Schleiermacher, Jean Paul, Clemens Brentano and Ludwig Tieck.

What we see here in this and other salons is a democratic spirit that gave their habitués a pre-taste of what the future might hold in society as such. It gave them a goal towards which their conversations could be aimed.

The role that Rahel Varnhagen's salon played in Berlin could be performed in even more democratic circumstances. Thus, in Edinburgh, the leading figures of the Scottish Enlightenment met to exchange views in basements given over to oyster parties and amid carousing into which the 'oyster wenches' also entered. The step, socially as well as physically, from the privacy, whether of salon or saloon, to open debate was therefore but a small one. The coffee-house, into which anyone with the will, education and interest could enter in order to join in conversation on the burning issues of the day, was virtually next door. Enlarged by its close links with journalism, as well as the theatre and literature generally, this public space became the precursor of the enormously more complex and infinitely less transparent public sphere we know today.

In this way, it is tempting to see in the genesis of the notion of a public sphere something larger already at work:

the possibility of the realization of an ideal in which the activity of the state can in principle be monitored and directed by informed, critical and public discourse. If at first not the discourse of all the governed, in these beginnings at least it was the discourse of those who had the good of all the governed as their professed political aim.

But why should we believe this? The ability of a bourgeois society to free itself from a system of governmental rule ill-suited to its expanding mercantile interests might lead one to suppose something else: that this was at heart simply a contest in which a new authority with its own ambitions sought to replace the old. That the spokesmen of the new society should be assisting a process whereby authority itself was on the way to being invested in 'the people' may seem an unlikely turn.

It is indeed conceivable that, if left to themselves, the bourgeoisie might have assumed the role of an alternative absolute authority, a growing but private elite steered by what they called 'reason' but which was in fact a version of rationality based on the background of their own commercial conceptions regarding the best way to run public affairs – the need, for example, to expand the moneyed class. On this view, when it became possible for anyone competent to join in such discussion, but due to the limits of literacy and education, competence itself was not just anyone's, the reasons discussion centred around concerns shared with those still excluded were more or less subtly commercial, rather than straightforwardly democratic. Least subtly, it was less a matter of spreading knowledge and freedom than of increasing buying power by filling more pockets with purses.

A reason why this was not exactly the case is the part still played precisely by authority. Not institutionalized authority of the kind now being undermined, along with its ties to religion and the idea of divine right; rather it was the authority of a climate of opinion shared among an increasingly influential class. But the climate itself was generated by, and generated in turn, its own authorities – a group of exceptionally talented writers. The climate was humanistic and basically secular and the writers collected under the title of the Augustan Age, the name echoing that of the age of the Emperor Augustus in Rome (27 BC–AD 14), famed for such poets as Horace, Ovid and Virgil. England and France both had their Augustan ages. The latter's preceded the former's and took place in an earlier era as far as the transition from political absolutism to bourgeois society is concerned. In late seventeenth-century France, Corneille enjoyed the patronage of Richelieu, one of whose principal aims was to bring the French population under the heel of the Bourbon monarchy. Molière was patronized by the King himself. But it would be a mistake to see Dryden's appointments in England as Poet Laureate and Historiographer Royal in the same light; he held them at a time when limited monarchy was no longer just a prayer. The events, beginning as they did with James II's abdication, and manner of the succession by William and Mary in the Glorious Revolution of 1688–9 both testify to this.[4] Politically focused writers such as Dryden, Defoe, Pope, Addison, Swift and Steele were the natural background of others such as Samuel Richardson and Henry Fielding, though also Defoe himself, who, by cultivating in the novel a less openly provocative form of critique, social as well as political, escaped the kinds of risk (censorship, imprisonment, exile) to which political satirists exposed themselves. They were also the background and precursor to philosophers such as John Locke and that avowed seeker of literary fame, David Hume. That Locke and Hume became influential political writers, formulating the principles of humane, self-governing societies, owed as much to the accessibility of their writings as to the way their thoughts gave shape to the new climate of opinion. For which of course we may thank the literary virtues they inherited from the classicist period.[5] It is important also to realize what might be called the general nature of philosophical or political discussion at the time. Although literary circles discussed literary matters, just as learned societies discussed science, the clear boundaries today dividing and delimiting these areas were not yet in place. Just as science could consort with religion, so could literary circles involve themselves in politics. One simple reason was the way that literature itself had taken on a critical role, not just in satire but also in portraying society in the novel (Richardson and Fielding). It was as natural for literary circles as for writers themselves to depict and, in doing so, implicitly comment on social life, thus engaging conversationally in politics.

When amplified by this documentary form of fiction and a developing journalism, such conversations could be easily perceived as a threat to the entrenched monopoly of church and state authorities in matters of common concern. In France and in the principalities and duchies of Germany things moved along more slowly and less smoothly. There, such threats would naturally provoke the authorities into enforcing their already existing powers of censorship. The example of Immanuel Kant provides a rather different illustration of the emergence of alternative sources of political authority.

Kant's views on matters of principle commanded wide respect and were taken seriously by government and governed alike. In the early 1790s Kant was accorded such respect as an authority on politics and morals that his every word on these topics was waited upon – either eagerly or anxiously. He had earlier had some brushes with authority; his lectures were monitored on account of their allegedly subversive anti-religious bias, and an essay by Kant was actually forbidden publication. The government was particularly interested in what this well-established champion of human freedom would say on the French Revolution. He had once earlier expressed support for the revolution, but the Prussian government would look amiss at any reasoned support of revolution. So, as a commentator put it, 'Kant's philosophy stood trial before the government'.[6]

However, considering the standing of the contestants, the trial naturally commanded a wider audience and also a wider jury. First, the jury would comprise several groups: those colleagues and critics at home and abroad who were opposed to Kantian rationalism, especially in ethics and religion, as well as a larger circle of those who, unable to take part in the contest or even properly to grasp the principles at issue, had a personal interest in the outcome of this potential conflict between perhaps the most eminent living representative of the Enlightenment and a repressive government armed with powers of censorship. For Kant to confirm his defence of the revolution would be to raise the alarm in the government, while to those who did have some grasp of the principles of the Kantian philosophy, an attack on it would seem a violation of them. Thus, as the same commentator also says, Kant stood on trial not just before the government but also 'before the public'.[7]

Several things can be learned from the example. First, it shows how easy it is for the *people*, those whose interests are allegedly at stake, to figure as the *topic* of politically oriented debate in the public sphere rather than as its participants.

Second, although as we think of it today at least in political respects the *public* is officially cast in a participatory role, the example shows what we anticipated earlier: how easily this public splits into two: *experts* on the one hand and interested *spectators* on the other. Just as the possible patrons of expensive architects form an immediate public for the architects themselves, while a wider public – still theirs – is formed of those affected in one way or another by what they succeed in having built, so Kant's public was formed in the first instance by those in a position either to 'buy' his philosophy or to reject it, and then of a wider circle of those personally interested in what a man of authority and influence had to say.

Today, of course, the public commanded by Kant is a thing of the past, and if Kant can be said to have any public today, it consists largely of students, commentators and followers who devote themselves to mastering the intricacies of this great thinker's thought.

Kant's way out of his dilemma was to defend the principles of the revolution but not the methods employed. Our commentator's verdict is that this was not just a piece of situation-saving casuistry on Kant's part but in the service of a higher ideal: freedom of the press.[8] If Kant may seem at first glance to have extricated himself from a nasty situation by engaging in something so contrary to his philosophy as a form of negotiation or compromise, there is another way of looking at it. The distinction between what a government proclaims as its ideals and the actual means it adopts to achieve them is a vital practical one and central to Kant's moral philosophy. What we can see Kant primarily doing here is addressing a government whose conservative ideals may not be reprehensible in themselves, but whose repressive means of resisting reform were a dereliction of its duties to the people. Censorship was the most obvious case of such repression. As Kant said in another place, and with no suggestion of compromise: 'Freedom of the pen is the only safeguard of the rights of the people.'[9]

Censorship, along with the kind of government that employs it, is no longer part of the default style of rule. It is reverted to in emergencies real and alleged, but generally in conditions that can be made acceptable to the public, and always with the proviso that it be limited and retracted as soon as conditions allow. This is part of a wider change regarding authority. Intellectual genius is no longer respected as a source of moral authority, guidance in this respect either being left to traditional beliefs or made a matter of individual conscience, though the latter often mediated by the corrupting influence of leaders of religious and other sects.

Freedom from authority and the campaign waged by writers for 'freedom of the pen' merge in the concept of a public sphere. As the space in which matters of common concern can be openly discussed and accepted as having a legitimate influence on government policies, the public sphere looks as if it should be the cornerstone of a democratic society. Yet questions remain about this public sphere. Among the more fundamental is the question of where to look for the answers. Is there still some authority to appeal to at least on this matter?

An obvious question is who is to take part. In the beginning that was decided by the participants themselves, or by their backgrounds, which were of a fairly uniform nature. They were sharers in a progressive culture which had its aims defined for it by the forms of government that then existed and by the limitations imposed both on open debate and, just as importantly, education. To form any kind of public sphere, freedom of the press and of speech were obvious first requirements. But the idea that *everyone* should participate on equal terms in the discussing and ordering of these affairs was no part of the original plan. Indeed, a main motivation for establishing the public sphere at all on this small scale was to take into account the accepted impossibility at the time of everyone shifting politically for themselves. The first thing these fledgling public spheres had to do was fend for themselves. The first priorities, before entering into questions of political organization, were the freedoms of speech and of the printed word for the already literate and educated, as Kant clearly saw. Unless the liberal messages that resulted from their debates could be broadcast and could find a public beyond the limited circles in which they occurred, they could hardly be expected to help further the expectations of the population at large. The question of how to incorporate this population into political debate itself was another matter.

An influential answer to this question has been offered by Habermas. In the notion of an ideal speech situation, he attempted to pinpoint and thus allow for factors that prevent people arriving at balanced judgements. The project presupposes that participants in debate have the required background knowledge and mental ability. The point is that they can still be hampered by the grip of an ideology or some inner hang-up. An ideal speech situation is one where all participants are freed of repressive mechanisms, social and psychological, that might muzzle or distort the appreciation of what others say. A tall order, as everyone including Habermas would admit. But is it a good answer, or is it a rationalist's answer, or, if so, is the fact of it being a rationalist's answer a reason for general agreement about it being a good answer, even the right one?

Whatever conclusions one draws concerning Habermas's views on what the public sphere should be, there is less controversy concerning what it is. We can at least all be agreed that, compared with the times of its origins, the public sphere, its composition and aims are today incomparably less transparent. Put starkly, it is a commercialized arena in which debate is hard to distinguish from entertainment, a space which, unlike its modest progenitor, offers not so much ever-wider opportunities for serious debate as an expanding billboard on which economic and partisan interests compete with each other for the private individual's custom. The vacuum left by the absence of central authority, whether governmental or intellectual, tends easily to be filled by a variety of role models or, in the case of religious sects and their ilk, by rigid group disciplines. Authority has not disappeared, it has merely changed its face. It manifests itself in rhetoric and defends itself, as well as whatever hard measures it decides to take, including censorship, in the name of expertise and information from protected sources. It is in the nature of the case, including as it does a natural capacity to invent technologies of communication, that in political matters audiences far outstrip participants. The public, as we have said, if or when it is anything, is typically an audience. It holds at best a watching brief.

Yet the ideals which gave birth to the public *sphere* were inherently of a participatory kind, and an essential element in sharing an interest in the public good was a common interest in *discussing* that good. Originally, the circles spoke to a public limited to the literate. Yet inevitably, and as literacy, more particularly political literacy, increased, they became producers with an audience, the *public* referred to by Habermas in the quotation at the beginning of this chapter – reading, watching, listening – playing the part of consumers, a role that in the end can embrace 'the public' as a whole.

In this there seems to be something inevitable. As a would-be player, or play space, on the political scene the public sphere appears doomed to become a sphere of what we earlier referred to as anonymous 'anyones'. This is already implicit in the 'eclipse' of the public, referred to by Dewey, though he also saw it as a crystallization into separate worlds of interest with their correspondingly mutually independent 'publics'. The problem is sheer size; the larger the nation, the more information and the wider the perspective required of those who would guide its future. Correspondingly the increasingly ill-equipped the private citizen to take on that task. The political theorist and columnist Walter Lippmann attacked those who still thought the public could be educated to the task and who clung to theories of popular government. He wrote that such theory 'rests upon the belief that there is a public which directs the course of events', while this public is 'a mere phantom . . . [and] an abstraction'.[10]

Curiously, the very same words were used by Søren Kierkegaard almost a century earlier. But he used them with a difference that is worth dwelling on. The phantom Kierkegaard refers to was a notional and non-obligating replacement for the active groupings of times gone (nations, city-states, factions, clans), in which the group itself was accountable to others for the actions of its individual members and the latter in turn responsible individually to the group. In a world no longer supporting the kind of dynamism in which it was natural for such groups to operate, and in which they found their active place, individuals are left, bare-headed as it were, to make their own judgements and to account for their own actions and views. But, exposed in this way in their singularity, these individuals seek a surrogate cover. It is the public; and both it and the appearance it gives of being some actual grouping are a sham created by the press. It is, says Kierkegaard, 'only when no energetic association gives substance to the concretion that the press creates this abstraction, the public, composed as it is of unreal individuals who are not and never can be united in the contemporaneousness of a situation or organization, and who nevertheless, it is insisted, are a whole'. Kierkegaard remarks, in the same place, that the public is a concept that cannot possibly occur in antiquity, for then 'a people itself had to appear *en masse, in corpore*, at the scene of the action . . .'. This substitute, limitless phantom-grouping, the public, appears nowhere, 'it makes for no situation and no assembly', and 'as you would expect, the abstraction formed paralogistically by individuals, instead of helping them, makes them recoil from one another'.[11]

Lippmann's 'mere phantom' is more in the nature of an impossible ideal. The ideal as well as its impossibility arise from the distance that exists in modern societies between the governing and the governed. He says, 'The private citizen today has come to feel rather like a deaf spectator in the back row, who ought to keep his mind on the mystery off there, but cannot quite manage to keep awake'.[12] What Lippmann, like Dewey, had in mind was the complexity of the modern commonwealth and the breadth of vision required to make informed political decisions. As we noted, Dewey was thinking from the perspective of a settler nation that has to organize itself without help or hindrance of local tradition, and he saw the public as originally a self-established entity in relation to a state that it had itself put in place. Expansion from small and local beginnings took this public out of its depth. Lippmann, speaking of various supposed remedies ('eugenic, educational, ethical, populist, and socialist') for this situation, says that 'all [these remedies] assume that either the voters are inherently competent to direct the course of affairs or that they are making progress toward such an ideal'. He says, 'I think it is a false ideal. I do not mean an undesirable ideal. I mean an unattainable ideal, bad only in the sense that it is bad for a fat man to try to be a ballet dancer.' Further, 'The individual man does not have opinions on all public affairs . . . there is not the least reason for thinking, as mystical democrats have thought, that the compounding of individual ignorances in masses of people can produce a continuous directing force in public affairs.'[13]

Dewey, an advocate of progressive education, was cautiously optimistic on behalf of participatory democracy, seeing some promise of a public able to understand and monitor the explanations of expert administrators. Lippmann for his part was unremittingly pessimistic; participatory democracy was a romantic dream. Whatever possible grounds there may be today for cautious optimism or a qualified scepticism, in any society even faintly resembling our own, it is surely indisputable that the possibility of a public formed of 'perfect citizens' is a thing of the past.[14] What we educate nowadays are specialists able to fill roles in a complex economic machine. There is, indeed, a factor that might have drawn Lippmann and Dewey closer together had they lived through recent events. We will draw attention to it later. In anticipation let us refer to another feature of modern society these early twentieth-century writers failed to foresee but which is now evident to everyone.

Lippmann distinguishes 'insiders', as expert administrators and economic experts able to 'make decisions', from 'outsiders', those who form the public. While the former are 'so placed' that they can 'understand and act', the outsiders are as if 'trying to navigate the ship from dry land'. They are 'necessarily ignorant, usually irrelevant and often meddlesome'.[15] But today Lippmann's insiders are themselves outsiders in respect of a system or network of interests in respect of which they too are outsiders, a system or network by which they are at any rate constrained. All this has been noted and discussed in detail by political philosophers, as well as by political commentators.

An important voice here is Habermas's. He speaks, as we know, for a democratic society in which citizens have access to political debate and can themselves be heard in it. To him the problem is one of communication. He points accordingly to the communicative infrastructure of society as the area (or collection of areas) crucially undermined by commercial forces. It is these that hinder free and open, or rational, debate. To correct the situation he proposes that the influence of those areas of life coordinated by communication should be widened, and in particular he suggests, as one commentator has put it, that we 'subordinate economic and administrative subsystems to decisions arrived at in open, critical, public debate'.[16]

There seems an obvious problem here. The 'we' who subordinate these subsystems to such debate must be a public already freed from the inhibiting influence of the commercialized media, or at least recruited from an otherwise passive public in sufficient numbers to acquire enough influence to counter those commercial forces. In short, how could an open and critical public debate that is effective in controlling the influence of commercial forces on the media be staged unless the communicative infrastructure had already been 'humanized' (as it is often put)? Indeed, the presence of open, critical debate in a world where the media are so essential to 'mediating' that debate, would indicate that the obstructive subsystems had already been brought under 'human' control. If humanizing and expanding the communicational infrastructure have to come first, what hope is there of that so long as the mass media continue to feed off their willing public?

As our brief references to Dewey and Lippmann already indicate, the idea of an open and critical debate on public matters in a large society is itself problematic. It isn't just the numbers, or the problem of coordinating a multitude of local debates. That presupposes that the insider/outsider distinction can be overcome. But in a modern society how can that ever be a realistic aim? That it is not so might have been discerned in the very origins of the idea of the public sphere.

The coffee-house debates cannot be treated as microcosmic versions of a nationwide debating forum where the public can be heard speaking for itself. They were indeed merely relocated extensions of the discussions held in the privacy of the salons. Wherever the discussions took place, due to their position the debaters were in a sense already virtual politicians and insiders. It would be nearer the letter and spirit of the coffee-house origins of public debate to say that, far from aiming to eradicate the outsider/insider distinction, such debate essentially presupposed it. It is true, as we noted, that those who met there spoke, in a public spirit, for those who for several reasons were not there; and also true that those absent included the many who lacked the education to take part. But suppose they had acquired it. The problem would not be merely one of space, though that is one side. More to the point, even if there had been space a conversation on such a scale would have ceased to be edifying, speaking, as it would have, across borders of experience and expertise. A conversation of all with all would need its own Hobbes and a Leviathan to bring order out of chaos. That in itself urges on us the need for another solution.

# **Four**

Our newspapers speak to us as much of public opinion as they do of the public whose opinion it supposedly is. And there seems no getting away from the fact that there is such a thing. It is easily outraged, sometimes upset, politicians appeal to it, try to influence it, we ourselves often side with it against our politicians. We, the public, were horrified by photographs of torture in the Abu Ghraib prison. Our horror might have some effect on the conduct of affairs. Documentaries on famine and other, nearer-to-home injustices may sometimes do more than just leave us alone with our feelings of impotence and loss of hope; they may also help to create climates of opinion that, if too late for many, have some effect on the future by forcing the hands of leaders sensitive to how 'the public' thinks.

But how can an entity as diffuse as the public think at all? Further, if it did, why should its views be taken seriously? As outsiders, we, the public, are just not well-enough informed on a wide-enough range of politically relevant topics to see what needs to be done on the political front. To let public opinion decide would be like trying to navigate the ship from the shore. National referenda may be an exception, but the only other familiar scenario is revolution.

Yet even Lippmann allows that there is such a thing as

public opinion. He claims moreover that it serves a useful political function. That function? He calls it the neutralization of force. Lippmann sees the mobilization of public opinion in times of crisis as helping to restore things to normal, bringing us back to that 'habitual process of life' in which we 'live and let live'.[1]

An important proviso is that the public at such 'junctures' delivers its opinion only on matters of the kind that can properly concern it. Although Lippmann does not quite say so himself, these concerns may be assumed to be of a general kind, topics that you do not need to be an insider to appreciate. In these cases, then, insiders may no longer disparage the opinion of outsiders. Developing this idea further, though probably beyond anything Lippmann had in mind, we might take these concerns to have a moral component, or, better, to embrace what comes within the broad compass of what Charles Taylor has recently discussed under the label 'social imaginary'. Our social imaginary is 'the way our contemporaries imagine the societies they inhabit and sustain'. Taylor offers an account of how our own imaginary comes to embrace a 'new conception of the moral order of society'. The latter, he says, has its source in the 'minds of influential thinkers'.[2] They provide a conception of order that gradually filters down into the various levels of society, until the conception itself becomes more or less integral to the way in which we think of ourselves, insiders and outsiders alike.

This chapter combines two thoughts from the above. One is that public opinion does indeed function in something like the way Lippmann proposes; there are critical junctures in the otherwise normal lives of a society when we may talk appropriately of the way or ways in which its public thinks. The other thought is the role of the writer, and the press.

These can alert people to things which may draw them together in forming an opinion. What Lippmann does not say is that, beyond disturbances in an otherwise stable way of life, the sight of visible injustice even in the normal course of events can also arouse the public's anger. In general, public opinion can serve just as well to undermine a stable status quo as to restore it.

The goal of stable society has guided the thinking of every political thinker from Plato to Rawls. One solution is to try to prevent instability from the start, another is to 'neutralize' it when it occurs. Among the neutralizers is the Scottish philosopher, David Hume, a writer who antedated the arrival of the public as we know it, but whose attempt to find a way of dealing with popular sentiment affords us an excellent opportunity to disassemble the notion of public opinion into its components and its antecedents and to reconstruct it in what can be offered as a theory of public opinion, positioning it in the political space of societies such as our own.

In 1742, Hume published an essay collection, *Essays Moral and Political*. It included a short piece entitled 'Idea of a Perfect Commonwealth'. Hume presented his proposal in 'as few words as possible', since '[a] long dissertation on that head would not . . . be very acceptable to the public'. His public, in this case one that would 'be apt to regard such disquisition both as useless and chimerical',[3] would be readers able to respond to the solid good sense and acid realism of Hume's proposals. They could listen without having to enter into learned and abstract discussion of the principles on which the proposals were based. Since these principles were in any case of a strongly utilitarian kind that would appeal to a general public without further argument, nothing essential was omitted. The essay is an excellent exercise in didactic journalism directed at the desirability of introducing a more limited monarchy into British government, a matter of interest wide enough at that time to command an audience, or a public. It attempts, democratically, to speak to the reason of a far wider circle than Kant could have expected to reach fifty years later.

In due course Hume's public came to include many others to whom his proposals and reflections must have seemed even more relevant. The Virginian-born James Madison incorporated some of them in his 'Notes on the Confederacy' published in 1787 over ten years after Hume's death.[4] Madison himself, one of the framers of the American constitution and collaborator in the *Federalist Papers*, became the fourth US President (1809–17).

The relevance of Hume's remarks for the American constitution is to be found in what he had to say on establishing a commonwealth 'in an extensive country'. Concern for effective democratic procedures might seem to dictate proximity; the voices of the distant are hard to hear, sometimes conveniently so for those not partial to what they say, but regrettably in the light of the ideal that everyone has a right not just to speak but also to be heard. Against this 'common opinion', as he calls it, Hume argues that distance acts as a useful barrier to the kind of popular turmoil that impedes piecemeal democratic progress. For if 'modelled with masterly skill', he says, a 'large government' allows 'compass and room enough to refine the democracy',[5] that is to say, to correct any undemocratic tendency due to sheer size. The model he recommends has local voters electing representatives to their county, these in turn electing magistrates for their own counties and a senator. It is the senators, who meet in the capital, who are 'endowed with the whole executive power of the commonwealth'.[6]

This hierarchical system of transference of power, in order to work as an instrument of piecemeal democratic reform, had to be protected from disruptive elements. Populism was a main source of disruption. Giving scope to a higher magistrate's personal appeal gives him greater political leverage than is due on the basis of the constituency he officially represents. Alternatively, the members of the constituencies might form larger de facto constituencies on their own, making the commonwealth bottom-heavy, a weakness in any political system. Democracies, says Hume, 'are turbulent' and, however much the people are organized into small groups as voters or representatives, their 'near habitation in a city will always make the force of popular tides and currents very sensible'. The advantage of a government whose 'parts' are sufficiently 'distant and remote' is that 'it is very difficult, either by intrigue, prejudice, or passion, to hurry them into measures against the public interest'.[7]

Since Hume's time, modern travel, the expanding media and the unlimited embrace of cyberspace have enabled even the largest commonwealths to approximate the conditions of near habitation. But another kind of remoteness must be considered: cultural diversity due to large-scale immigration. On '[t]he stream of immigrants that has poured in', Dewey remarks that it 'is so large and heterogeneous that under conditions which formerly obtained it would have disrupted any semblance of unity as surely as the migratory invasion of alien hordes once upset the social equilibrium of the European continent'.[8] We may ask whether any unity is now due as much to the diversity as to its lack. Cities, too, have changed immensely since the mid-eighteenth century, both in size and composition. Cultural diversity and distance are a defining feature of the modern metropolis. Strangely, on Hume's own assumption, they seem to form excellently stable common-wealths in their own right. But leaving aside possible amendments to Hume's premises, what we need to consider is the assumption that what Hume calls popular tides and currents work against the public interest.

In describing such tides and currents in terms of force, Hume suggests that popular movements resemble in some way forces of nature. They are not the work of reason. Like raging torrents, they need to be resisted or contained if political reason is to prevail. The metaphor of tides and currents brings to mind attitudes and tendencies subject to outside influence rather than as self-generated drives from within the body politic. Tides change as do currents, in strength as well as direction. Hume thinks such tendencies in the population at large are divisive as well as disruptive: 'Although it is more difficult to form a republican government in an extensive country than in a city, there is more facility, when once it is formed, of preserving it steady and uniform without tumult and faction'.[9]

Though aimed at a lay audience, Hume's proposals for the democratic state are still typical of the philosopher. This commonwealth has a top-down structure with reason in control, though a reason disseminated as widely as possible but with safeguards against unruly intervention from below. Admittedly the reason is not that of a rationalist philosopher. Hume appeals to a general consensus that people will arrive at on their own authority once the point has been made clearly enough to them. A companion essay, 'Of Original Contract', ends by appealing to general opinion. There is 'in all questions with regard to morals, as well as criticism', says Hume, 'no other standard by which any controversy can be decided'.[10] Hume is optimistic about the ability of people in general to arrive at common-sensical conclusions, given the right conditions for doing so. One of these is that the conclusions be shorn of unnecessary intellectual trappings. Hume's 'Idea of a Perfect Commonwealth' is itself tailor-made to elicit just the kind of assent that he expects of reasonable people in the right setting. Such assent differs from the popular, or populist, views which Hume thinks must be prevented from taking effect, if not also forming.

The populism Hume refers to is not what we would call public opinion. But then neither is Hume's 'general opinion' that. It is not the former, because what we refer to as public opinion, whatever its content, would not generally be regarded as a threat to the state as such; if critical it would be at most a threat to a sitting government. As we are well aware, it can just as well support the government. Nor is it the latter, because in Hume's day general opinion was still confined to an educated elite able to appreciate the kind of problems with which the essay on a perfect commonwealth deals and to judge the persuasiveness of Hume's proposed solutions.

According to one writer, it was Voltaire who just a little later 'invented' the idea of public opinion, or, as he says, 'virtually' invented it. We must look at both the claim and the qualification.[11]

By the time Hume's essay appeared, Voltaire was Europe's most widely read author and playwright. But he also became a controversial and frenetically energetic polemicist in the cause of free-thinking. Although his faith in good sense was as great as Hume's, while Hume was concerned mainly to assert, against the rationalists, that good sense was good enough and in any case all we had, Voltaire went out of his way to attack those institutions that prohibited its free play. Besides his literary activities, Voltaire was also something of a seasoned politician, having been personal adviser to Frederick the Great. Home from his political exploits abroad, he became a notorious political satirist and pamphleteer. In 1762, Voltaire was approached by the widow of one Jean Calas, a leading textile merchant in Toulouse.[12] Calas had been convicted on suspicion of murdering his son and brutally broken on the wheel. Voltaire who, as our commentator points out, had never produced the kind of systematic work that would earn him a place in the pantheon of philosophers, but whose 'already long career had been made up in good part of looking for the right way to force the hand of governments', seized this opportunity to indulge his passionate interest in reform. Convinced, after due investigation, that a grave injustice had been perpetrated, Voltaire took personal charge of the Calas case and 'began pouring out a torrent of words in all directions'.[13]

One important factor is that, like Hume, Voltaire kept his arguments at a level where ordinary literate people would understand them and see their point – one reason why people may have failed to acknowledge him as a bona fide philosopher. Second, however, and quite unlike Hume, Voltaire exploited actual examples of glaring injustice to generate opposition to the system of government that was able to perpetrate them. If this is where the notion was born then public opinion is already, in its origins, a political notion. Its clear connections with what would become political journalism are also evident. As Saul says, Voltaire 'developed the idea that specific, heart-rending cases could be converted into great battles which would set standards and force widespread reform'.[14] One might say, in words he himself would not have chosen, that in his hard-fought campaign against fanaticism, Voltaire succeeded in clearing a space for the democratic exercise of good sound sense, the space we now refer to as the 'public sphere'. He himself, a spokesman for the enlightened middle classes rather than principled enemy of monarchical government, would have regarded it rather as a matter of defending freedom of thought and religious tolerance against tyranny and bigotry.[15]

But if the public belongs originally to a politically focused ambience in which the individual stands in the centre and enjoys certain rights of protection from the state, the opinion that Voltaire aroused crossed state borders. Two factors were at work here: the literary fame that had already given him an international audience and the nature of the causes he chose to champion. Injustice at the hands of the powers that be is a cause close to the hearts of the people of most nations and, we may assume, especially so at a time when potentially democratic procedures of the kind Hume drafted were, if not indeed utopian, for many nations still a thing of the future. Thus Voltaire, for the battles he was in a position to generate, could, as Saul puts it, mobilize a vast 'army'. As we know, Voltaire was by no means the first writer to engage his readers on a political front. Nor, as Zola's decisive defence of Alfred Dreyfus in 1898 testifies, is the tradition confined to pre-democratic states. But, given reservations still to be discussed about what it means to talk of public opinion, Voltaire was certainly the first to command a politically engaged audience wide enough to warrant identifying the source of the support he received as that of a population comparable with what we nowadays refer to as the public.

The example of Voltaire provides clear support for the notion of public opinion as that of an audience someone is able to capture by highlighting and provoking interest in a certain topic. In the case cited the topic was injustice. Given the circumstances of the time, Voltaire was able to impart, to a wide audience already disposed both to read him and to react to tales of injustice close to home, his own concern with examples of injustice, examples that he was in a special position to make conspicuous. Were we looking for some general definition of public opinion, we might do worse than begin by saying that it is, in the form of a currently adopted attitude or belief, a manifestation of a set of ready-formed dispositions to respond to some respected source of information.

It is nevertheless true that we typically employ the notion of public opinion in the context of national politics. That is no doubt because it is a vital factor in the survival of our own governments. But the fact does not prevent our saying that public opinion, even there, deserves its name just as much because it is an opinion made public as because it is the opinion of the public. We can say that public opinion consists in dispositions to listen to respected sources. Saying that dispositions are to be found in the public is not the same as saying that they are the dispositions of this public. The dispositions are those of individuals in this or that population, in this case the population that forms the public. They consist in a readiness among a fair number of citizens to respond to issues close to home: abortion, social welfare, environmental and economic issues, national security, even who should coach the national football team. There would be nothing wrong in saying that these were responses of the public, but saying it must not be taken to infer that the opinion is one necessarily confined to 'the public'; many issues, especially injustice, are close to home in a sense that is not dependent on national identities. Again, of course, we might want to say that in such cases it is just a wider public that forms 'the public', and it is this wider public that has the opinion. But then we would have ceased to treat the idea of the public as a component in a state, or at most it would be to treat wider units than actual states as political. It might even be taken as shorthand for a combination of actual states. Rather than any of these, we are preferring the alternative: public opinion is so called because it is an opinion that has captured a public, its own public.

Nevertheless, for public opinion to carry the political weight we know that it does, something more seems needed. In the first place, politicians respond to public opinion only because they themselves know or at least believe that a significant number of people hold the relevant beliefs. Second, they might care considerably less about the fact that these beliefs were held in whatever numbers if they supposed that those individuals who held them did not know that other individuals did so as well. Thus it is only when individual voices combine into a single *vox populi* that anything called public opinion can have any political weight. A little cynically, one might even claim that in many cases, unless they knew that others held the belief, those holding the belief would themselves be less likely to do so, certainly less likely to voice it. However that may be, all this indicates that there is yet another sense of 'public' at work in our notion of public opinion, namely 'public' in the sense of 'open', that is, as a voice, or a unison chorus, audible to all able to listen in the public sphere.

That is what we should expect. Public opinion is opinion made public. It is also the opinion of many people. One normal and quite natural way of putting this is to say it is the opinion of the public. But what has been argued here tells against the idea that there is a public and that it forms an opinion.

There is much to be said for an alternative idea: opinions

conveyed to the public generate audiences for those opinions. This is not to say that individuals form their views about public policy only by being part of an audience that responds to the views as they are already articulated in the public sphere. Some do not do that; they form their views or at least their formulations of them in private. Some may even take time and trouble to sift out what they themselves think. But that in general is not the way in which what we refer to as public opinion comes about. Whatever individual citizens believe about matters of public concern (and the fact that public opinion typically concerns itself with public affairs adds yet another 'public' flavour to the notion), whenever there is something to refer to as public opinion, it is when something or someone sets people's minds in motion so that it registers on their political consciousness. The opinions set in motion are best described as propensities or dispositions, or better, as deep-seated and shared preferences that (calling to mind Hume's hydrographic metaphors) surface when suitably described events evoke them.

From this it may seem that public opinion comes closer to Hume's popular tides and currents, with their implications for tumult and faction, than to his 'general opinion'. Ideally, it would be better if it tended towards the latter. General opinion, as something to appeal to – as Hume himself appealed to it in presenting his criticism of the notion of an original contract – is not a set or repertoire of pre-established prefer-ences ready to be invoked on cue. It is the product of a state of mind congenial to making judgements, enabling individuals separately to arrive at common-sensical and just conclusions in context. Public opinion is, to the contrary, a set of disposi-tions to feel strongly about some topic that is brought to one's attention. Typically it comes ready formulated, so that the very expression of it, the way in which the public views its own preference, also has its origin there. True, having access to the public sphere, certain individuals can contribute both to what is made topical there and to how it is formulated. But mostly the case is as it was with Voltaire, if not on the same scale. Voltaire's voice was that of a super-celebrity able to arouse a popular response to his depictions of glaring injustice and social inequality within the political frame his depictions provided. Part, then, of what is implied in saying that Voltaire *invented* the idea of public opinion is the fact that the influence he exercised was precisely not due to his taking part as a member of an already formed public. As for his inventing it *virtually*, that may be understood in terms of the time in which Voltaire lived. Just as the public came into its own only with the establishing of a public sphere, so too with public opinion. It had to wait until it was possible to say, though mistakenly, that it is the opinion of that public.

It is important that Voltaire's authority and his ability to exercise it were expressions of the time. Two opposite perspectives help to identify that particular historical situation: a bottom-up or grass-roots perspective which discloses the historical conditions in which the topic of injustice was 'close to home' to so many, and a top-down perspective which notes the pervasive influence of Enlightenment thought at the time, and the way in which autocratic governments, by having the bases of their clerical as well as secular authority undermined, were gradually being forced to respond to public pressure.

A combination of the two offers a prospective view of that highly symbolic event, the storming of the Bastille on 14 July 1789, and the wide-ranging political, economic and social changes that resulted. These changes, though by no means the revolution that followed, to say nothing of the Terror, were if

not the fulfilment of Voltaire's own dream, at least consequences of the movement towards legal justice which is
where his passions were directed. It has been claimed that the
reason why political change in France, unlike Britain, took the
form of revolution was the characteristic appeal of the *philos-
ophes* to abstract reason, evident also in Voltaire but not Hume.
It set a goal of the regeneration of humankind that lay beyond
the capacity of ordinary people, with the result that these
were disdained as the 'masses', a majority of people incapable
of enlightenment.[16] The abstract reasoning gave rise to the
French Revolutionary concept of *citoyen* in which the individual
was thought of as personifying the state. Since the state
remains itself, actual individuals become abstract and replaceable. Conversely, the state becomes 'the individual'. Hume set
the tone of the British Enlightenment, with its more prosaic
and humane approach, when in introducing his own conception of a model commonwealth he said, 'All plans of government which suppose great reformation in the manners of
mankind are plainly imaginary.'[17]

Nowadays, due partly to the effects of the changes which
both enlightenments brought about, authority of the kind
Voltaire exercised can scarcely arise, or at any rate be wielded.
Again two factors can be noted. Due less to the changes themselves than to the motivating idea behind them, the
Enlightenment movement to which both Hume and Voltaire
in their different ways belonged contained a built-in demise
of such authority. The aim was to clear the way for free and
rational individuals capable of creating the conditions of a
free society, a society where tolerance and justice reigned. In
such a society there should be no reason for philosophers like
Kant or writers like Voltaire to be in possession of insights
other than those available to sound common sense.

Second, although injustice survives in western societies, the presence as part of these societies of an area in which wrongs can be advertised and pressure put on governments or local authorities to redress them means that the individuals in these societies are themselves now in principle able to bring such wrongs to public attention, the more easily because such things are now universally recognized *as* wrongs. The spotlight merely needs to be turned on or the whistle blown, though blowing the whistle has its personal costs and can cause new injustice. Ideally at least, we live in societies of the kind Hume envisaged, in which there is 'compass and room enough to refine the democracy'. They are societies in which the sensationalism that an exceptional writer like Voltaire could exploit has become the speciality of the journalist and mass media, not of individual literary talent.

What Enlightenment thinkers, optimistic about the authority that could be placed in the individual's powers of independent reasoning, did not see was the rising complexity of a society based on property-ownership. Initially, property-ownership was made a requirement of political participation because it entailed a personal investment in society. Hume's blueprint allowed only freeholders to be voters or representatives. These property-owners could be called the initial 'public', just because they had, as proprietors, an area in cash or kind of guaranteed privacy, from which they could then emerge in order to engage with one another in 'public life', that is to say, in deliberative and executive activity on behalf of the population as a whole. The liberal ideal of a public sphere was that everyone should somehow be included in this area. However, as the public grew, not just with the population but more importantly as the requirements of private citizenship (income and gender) were gradually relaxed, the further development of capitalism and the workings of the market led to new possibilities of injustice. In place of the ideal of a public sphere in which the state is effectively monitored by the governed, the state is now one among several factors in a field of forces that operate on both it and the public. The effect on the latter is, as noted in the previous chapter, to isolate it from the very regulatory system that on an account like Dewey's was its own invention. The public are effectively excluded from exerting any influence on this field of forces. Or rather, echoing Lippmann, the public as an entity remains only in the form of a phantom; largely depoliticized, not just by choice but by the barriers that prevent outsiders becoming insiders, what remains of the public in political terms is an amorphous assembly of clienteles, constituencies and lobbies.

It may seem a paradox that it is the political public that is on the way out at the very moment rational man (in a gender-neutral sense) is now supposedly in place, privacy secured by civil law, and the individual's judgemental authority guaranteed by virtue of there being no other recognized authority than sound common sense, the exercise of which is potentially open to all. But increasingly there is correspondingly little for this individual to decide, except when occasionally casting a vote or answering a questionnaire. Armed with a guarantee of freedom of movement in all public spaces, including some where the forces themselves can be seen or heard at work, or the results of their interplay put on view and publicly debated, all this individual has is at best, as we said earlier, a watching brief.

How could it be otherwise? This vast public itself could never form an assembly. This truth was carried to its logical conclusion by nineteenth-century anarchists, who believed the smaller the community the better the opportunity for an open and democratic life.[18] Although nowadays, given well-nigh universal education and limitless information, one can disagree with Hume's view that even in smaller populations '[i]f the people debate, all is confusion', and even if, given the possibility of televised discussions by well-informed people, we may no longer fear, as Hume did, that the matters in hand be not so much debated for their own sake as reduced to the platitudinous level of gossip and suggestion,[19] it is still hard to see where more *discussion* can lead in the quest for justice and the good life. More important, surely, is an ability to recognize and correct for the distortions that reach us in the discussions that already take place among insiders, and in the consequences to which their decisions lead.

In this respect we are in a position not unlike the one towards which Hume's remarks seem directed. Not unsurprisingly for a Tory, Hume makes an undemocratic-sounding remark, but his reason for making it appears less undemocratic. He refers to '[t]he lower sort of people and small proprietors' and says they are 'good enough judges of one not too distant from them in rank or habitation . . . and therefore, in their parochial meetings, will probably choose the best, or nearly the best representative [but] they are wholly unfit for county meetings, and for electing into the higher offices of the republic'. Why are they unfit? Because '[t]heir ignorance gives the grandees an opportunity of deceiving them'.[20]

Today, assuming perhaps unwisely that universal education has taken care of Hume's scruples, the growth of professional government and expertise has nevertheless introduced another kind of ignorance, and with it corresponding opportunities to deceive. The suggestion put forward here is that the way in which the public forms an opinion resembles that in which *aficionados* respond to works of art, or to the work of individual artists, pop groups, or different kinds of music. But playing on the feelings of the electorate is also an art, and politicians whose careers in current democratic societies depend on public support are nowadays well supported also by experts in the art of tweaking, tilting or 'spinning' accounts of the events they wish their constituencies, whether local or national, to respond to. They are able to play on feelings, of fear, insecurity, national pride, a sense of national mission. These people, the new grandees, have the advantage over their voters of an insider's comprehensive insight into the many interests that political life must cater to. Or, perhaps nearer the truth, the advantage they have is that of being able to produce their own simplified version of this insight for popular consumption. Another possibility, equally sinister, is that they do not have such a comprehensive insight and are in fact at the mercy of powers over which they themselves have no insight, or if insight, little control. In that case it is not they, but those controlling the forces of capital, who are the modern equivalent of Hume's grandees, and our own 'commonwealth' is an illusion. But the true grandees might also be the forces themselves, over which there is little if any control.

Whatever the case here, even if the public as such is excluded from political proceedings, it is clear that public opinion is vital to those proceedings. It is vital in the sense that those engaged in them require some backing for something the electorate should be able to take for granted, namely that it is the public's interests that they serve. However, it is equally clear from what has just been said that the public's opinion can be manipulated and even bought. Institutions formed in the days when free speech was still something to be fought for were intended as organs of public information and debate. Now they come under the general rubric of 'image management', one of whose branches is to manage consensus, another to promote a consumer culture that keeps the public busy with and increasingly addicted to its privacy.

# Five

In western societies privacy is at a premium. It is what people want and expect governments to provide. Historically that is strange since originally 'privacy' (in Latin *privatio*) meant 'deprivation', or more simply, 'privation'. Thus the sense of the predicate 'private' is originally that of having had something significant taken away. This would be the more obvious if the accent were put on the second syllable. For the Romans, privacy or being private straightforwardly meant being out of public office, or not yet in it. As Dewey notes, 'etymologically "private" is defined in opposition to "official"', and he adds, 'a private person being one deprived of public position'.[1] This sense lingers on only faintly today. Private members of the British House of Commons are not in public office but on the other hand private secretaries somehow are. Why is it, then, that in modern societies privacy has become almost a holy concept, something to live and die for, and certainly something everyone wants to keep?

Privacy was once classically defined as the 'general right to be let alone'.[2] The USA, more than any other nation, has underlined this right and protecting it is the generally accepted first aim of its government. So long as the private domain is secured, first of all behind the private front door or garden gate, but also the corporate portal, no one cares very much who does the governing. That is because an implicit plank in any party programme is that, even abroad, literally as well as merely beyond the front door, privacy is protected. The space of free and open debate 'out there' on matters of public concern is of course also of some importance, but only to the extent that it provides the public with assurances that it can safely pursue its legal private ends, legal to the extent that they do not impinge on similar protection provided for the neighbour. The public sector is a deliverer of services and security. When catastrophe occurs, as in September 2001, the first thought of the public is that the public sector should rally to protect it. In general, such a public is more sensitive to the ways in which firefighters, airport police, secret-service agencies, and so on, minimize threats to its private domain than to the composition and political attitudes of the government itself.

A population made to feel fearful for the safety of a privacy to which it is ideologically attached or in which it has a deep psychological investment, also lends a sympathetic ear to calls for stricter regulations to reinforce that safety, even at the cost of ideals of which the population boasts; the same goes for calls to arms in defence of the nation whose integrity is needed to provide protection for its private way of life. There is some hint of panic, or pathology, here, in the way that normal requirements of critical judgement are so easily set aside, and in the speed with which ideals dear to the population are overridden. The same is evident in a popular tendency to acquiesce in a government's policies of non-involvement when fears for the nation are not invoked. Such arguments as that intervention could make things worse, is likely to damage interests abroad or has too little voter support are widely accepted without further argument. If this in itself is too little to suggest something rotten in popular political psychology, it is at least evident that the centrality of privacy in western culture makes for clear weak spots, both in the society and in its system of government. Diverting attention away from the system of government itself, which is assigned a merely instrumental role, has the effect of emptying the public sphere and allowing its omnipresent re-occupation by a powerful controlling system that forms a private sphere of its own.

The situation has interesting parallels with one which a philosopher described some two hundred years ago. He spoke of a 'life . . . restricted to the proper maintenance of one's property, a contemplation and enjoyment of one's totally subservient little world'. He was characterizing the old regime in Germany, as he saw it a world made up of a multiplicity of private lives and no real public life. It was a particularistic world which offered no foothold for a sense of participation in a whole.[3] More especially, he saw the particularism carried over to government too. His criticism was that the state institutions which, in a well-organized state, should express the whole, and which the denizens of the private worlds could acquire a sense of in the services they performed for the public, in the old regime formed just another private world of its own, the isolated world of the rulers.

Not so different from the situation we have been describing? It may seem so. The old regime may have arrived there from another direction, and the solution that Hegel – for it was he – proposed may follow too closely the contours of the Prussian monarchy of his day to find wide support in ours. But one important similarity, however little obvious at first sight, is revealing. In an early aphorism Hegel remarked on what then were regarded as public spaces, complaining that they were 'no longer frequented'. He objected that having become 'bored by the public ... [o]n s'assemble en famille ...'. These spaces were 'balls, public places, the theatre'.[4]

In another comment on the 'privative' sense of the term 'private', Hannah Arendt has said more recently that '[t]o live an entirely private life means above all to be deprived of things essential to a truly human life'. Now, we might think, given our media world in which shared location means so little for communication, that what she takes us to have lost is presently well on the way to being restored. What we lose, she says, is 'the reality that comes from being seen and heard by others'. Losing that, she claims, deprives us of an 'objective' relationship with these others, one that 'comes from being related to and separated from them through the intermediary of a common world of things'.[5] But again, some may say that a practically unlimited world of things is now being made available to all on the Internet. There are even those who see the promise of a new kind of social reality in virtual communities in cyberspace.[6]

Quite apart from these possibilities made possible by media innovations, we can also point to a vast expansion nowadays, in both size and number, of the spaces where people actually do meet in public.

On closer inspection, however, no matter how crowded these spaces can be, they hardly provide that sense of conspicuous social celebration Hegel would have liked to find in the public places he saw deserted. Think of discothèques, pop concerts, football matches and even pedestrian precincts. Whatever sense of immersion in forms of collective enthusiasm or sheer release from loneliness these can offer, they provide nothing like the paradigms of social participation the young Hegel was referring to. In discos any genuine socializing is prohibited by the sheer level of noise; at pop concerts the crowd and heady atmosphere are simply part of the entertainment that each ticket-holder seeks for him- or herself – community spirit, if any, is a privilege of the fan club, though even there jealousies can tend to separate the membership. As for any incipient or actual sociality that may once have sought a footing in the streets and pavements, or bus stations and airport lounges for that matter, this is now effectively drained by a mobile-phone habit that not only turns people away from the space they share but, with its unnatural loudness, even disturbs all opportunity for silent soliloquy, or any sense of silent community, to say nothing of quiet conversation, among the technologically under-equipped.

This account may sound jaundiced. It will do so particularly to those who enjoy or contribute to forms and levels of community spirit that nevertheless survive in our world. To those it may be replied, however, that these, too, frequently take the form of private islands in a wider population. They certainly fall far short of what Hegel required of collective celebration. His way out of his uncollected archipelago of island-worlds, with the rulers occupying just another island, was to try to establish and vindicate a sense of deep national or political cohesion, felt even at the private level. Typically for him, he saw the promise of it in a feature of the unsatisfactory situation itself. This was the fervour with which people cultivated their particular worlds, an eagerness wholly out of proportion to what good sense would tell them these worlds could offer by way of fulfilled lives. It was a case of displaced energy, and carrying on as if these worlds themselves could provide such fulfilment was something Hegel called 'bad consciousness': a matter of treating what is merely ephemeral as though 'the absolute'.[7] Through increasing awareness of the conflict between means and end, a better idea of the nature of fulfilment would gradually find a footing.

However we judge Hegel's diagnosis and cure, we easily see how far modern life has outgrown whatever chances it may once have had of filling public spaces with anything like what Hegel found lacking there. For all its ubiquity, our public is politically anonymous. And in spite of attempts in theory and through media presentation to bring about the appearance of popular rule, it is hard to deny that rulers today are in practice as remote as in the old regime itself. There may be hidden bridges, but despite appearances, the traffic along them goes essentially in one direction.

Several significant developments distinguish our society from the one Hegel criticizes. First, any modern counterpart of the old regime must preserve the appearance of democracy. However, since the public is inclined in any case to leave things to the rulers, while the latter have the facilities to create the illusion that the public is nevertheless in on the game, the possibility remains that the actual situation differs less than it does on the surface. Second, unlike the private worlds of the late eighteenth century, ours have become sanctuaries from whose 'privacy' we are able to lead sedentary public lives all the same, socially as well as politically, simply by pressing buttons. We socialize from the sofa by telephone, we are members of various publics in the sense adumbrated earlier, by being entertained and sometimes educated as audiences of whatever gets piped into our homes. There is justification for the coinage 'infotainment', and the infotainers include the self-interested caretakers (as well as assassins) of political careers. Third, Hegel talks of people withdrawing from public life into their families. In his time these were the ultimate islands of (politically relevant) privacy. The organic unity formed by a family was a precursor of the rational form of organic unity that Hegel assumed would be provided by the state. Indeed marriage itself in the context of Hegelian society, besides calling for a socially binding divine blessing, also implied possession of private property. Property was not just a privilege, or a playground or a refuge from public life, but an ethical investment in an ongoing social order. It gave that order's inhabitants the power to influence the state on the state's terms, but also on their side the means collectively to express their humanity.[8] Without such an investment a person was merely an 'abstract' outsider – in a sense not far from Lippmann's except that for him it is a matter not of property but of expertise: what makes the outsider is the fact that the skills required to direct public affairs are beyond the ordinary citizen's reach.

Our world differs radically from the one Hegel envisaged. For one thing, our public space is one in which careers can be cut out, business empires built, travel and entertainment opportunities exploited, a place for adventure, competition and self-display. It is also the platform on which to enjoy the corresponding rewards, which include wealth, public acclaim, even stardom. And in a rental world of easy mobility, where ownership tends to be corporate and taxable real estate no longer the expression, or original site, it once was (or taken to be) of the individual's humanity, alternative fulfilments in this glittering world of ours seem everywhere available.

The reason why the bourgeoisie, according to Hegel anyway, withdrew into their privacies was a visible lack of real public life. The implication is that if a real public life existed they would have returned. What was needed to make public life real was a sense of participation in a concerted human project, a sense that it was reckoned a public space filled with public life should provide.

The picture of our own society is quite another. It is of a society in which privacy is protected from public life. Being private is what people want positively to be. Whatever interest there is in public life is more than satisfied by what is relayed to them in their homes. As for what lies outside, that is where the modern public seeks relief from the boredom of privacy confined to the home. Public space, both physical and abstract, is a playground to which it can escape but is in reality no more than an extension of its private sphere; the forms of fulfilment it offers have nothing evidently to do with *collective* expressions of humanity. In the forum or elsewhere, once in the great outdoors private citizens remain essentially private.

As for restoring private–public ties, even if that was desired the prospects would seem far more dismal to us than they did to Hegel. Within Prussia's small compass, Hegel could envisage reinstating a sense of participation in the whole by providing meaningful places in a state where a sense of its multi-participatory organization was also a part of the self-awareness of those who occupied the places. Under such conditions, in which membership had such a clear profile, it was easy to identify outsiders and to grasp in what way they were abstract. In 'larger' governments and a globalizing world it is first of all the 'community' and not the individual that becomes increasingly abstract.

But Hegelians would say that the priority here can be explained by the fact that our individual does not need increasingly to become abstract; in lacking an investment in the state the individual is that already. If outsiders were once fairly easy to detect – apart from the outlaws, they were those without fixed property, or at least those who might qualify as freeholders but for some reason owned no such property – in today's societies (and we are referring throughout only to western societies) no such obvious footholds are on offer to the public as such for a personal sense of participation and responsibility. We are then, in effect, at the outset, all of us outsiders. Worse, we are outsiders within an invisible network, but in respect of it we are insiders with no control. Instead of the citizen having an investment, the citizen *is* an investment, an investment handled by the economic powers that determine the safe future of the state, which in turn pampers and protects those privacies upon whose consumerist possibilities and habits its sponsors depend. In so far as the private citizen is the investment, what reaping the rewards of that investment requires is the continual expansion of the public space in which privacies can fruitfully but always still privately operate.

Privacy and the Media
# Six

The emptiness of public space goes together with the abstractness of the private citizen. They are indeed two sides of the same coin. What makes the individual abstract is lack of a sense of anything out of which it has grown and has its current being; what the space is emptied of are manifestations of allegiance to a nation state. Both absences are easily lost sight of in this pampering of the private citizen. There is so much 'out there' that can be done, things to be busy about, possibilities to realize. In order to grasp the abstractness we have to see what has been lost in the way of acquiring possibilities. Technology has brought to our fingertips a range of facile skills each of which we would earlier have had to rely on others to provide. Those who provided it, in order to have secured these skills, would have had to undergo a long and specialized apprenticeship. The abstraction, here, lies in this removal of opportunities to develop professional trade identities. Specialized skills rooted in local traditions were once recognizable niches that people could inhabit as respected servants of the community. Now that the 'skills' are universal, easy to acquire and learned from scratch, they come without roots. When we venture out into the world we have no background.

Second, learning from scratch is nowadays a feature of

education quite generally. It does not mean beginning at the beginning, as the expression suggests. It means programming education to introduce the pupil or student to a world of thought the main features of which are already fixed and lie there packaged ready for anyone to assimilate. To be effectively taught, a learner is first unburdened of whatever ideas or traditions are not in the package, and which might therefore stand in the way of the efficient programming that it is the aim of education itself to become. Thus what beginning from scratch means here, for those who do have backgrounds, is beginning over again. The result is that in the ever-growing numbers of multicultural nations there is a trend towards uniformity that requires at the same time the draining away of all ethnic and cultural diversity.

In the telltale media branch of a globalizing world, this abstraction is paraded as a virtue. It offers icons of a new global urbanity like that of the Armani-suited Master Card-carrying executive, equally at home in any conceivable environment. Should the thought of being a credit-card-carrying globetrotter versed in adult pleasure not appeal to us, other icons are available, for example, deserts and endless horizons for moody misfits. More poignant are those abstract advertisers' icons made from living public heroes. Any hint of personality these stars may or may not personally possess is studiously ignored to give place to the multiple consumer-directed poses in which they are made to appear. A clearer case of universality bought at the expense of personality would be hard to find.

The monetary metaphor is apt, now that the discussion enters upon the world of the media (film, television, radio, the Internet and the press). Today, though in its niche-supported version a thing of the past, personality is a highly marketable commodity, though what is meant by personality is something else: a public persona. Personae are not actual persons but masks behind which real persons are made to appear, or make themselves appear, before their audiences or publics. Personality in this sense is part of a vast and complex interchange between private and public, an interchange in which the public in its privacy seeks to escape public anonymity.

In the vacuum left by the unavailability of niche-supported personality, what is more natural than that, in searching for replacements, the abstract individual should look for opportunities in public space. We are reminded of the thought that public space offers itself as an arena where individuals may form audiences (in fact innumerable audiences or publics) and where, in a competitive minority of cases, they may also become the kind of public property – the word 'celebrity' comes to mind – that itself attracts audiences. Whatever else it may be besides, public space is a space of player-audience opportunities, and as one would expect of this particular relationship, it is a space that is biased heavily in favour of the audience.

There need be nothing sinister in that. An audience is not simply passive, and its members can learn as well as be entertained. We reminded ourselves earlier that there is something called audience participation and must bear in mind that audiences are formed in response to something that awakens in them. As for players, in our media-drenched world where web-site homes are readily available, in principle almost anyone in their search for an audience can indulge in this harmless form of self-advertisement. Some of the things that can go wrong have been extensively discussed through the years. One of them has to do with the distinction between what we are and how we appear to be to others. If a significant amount of pressure is put on people to sustain public masks but these deviate significantly from the persons they are to their friends and at home, or if the effort required to cultivate and sustain such masks means they have no real opportunity to acquire stable personalities of their own, with the consequence that the public persona takes over and does service as a private one, then the health of a society that produces such pressures may be put in question.

It is also widely agreed that in order to become reasonably stable selves privately, we need to be accepted and recognized by others for the qualities we acquire and on which our (quite complex) sense of who or what we are is built. Even if it is true that, as a rule, we inherit from our environment the expectations we have of ourselves, this potentially stabilizing fact can also prevent our raising ourselves to a level where any stability gained is due more to our own acceptance of ourselves in the roles than to the environment. The general point is that selfhood is contingent on the kinds of relationships a society provides and these are mirrored in, or as we could equally say, these mirror the state of the public/private nexus as it is found in a society at any given period. A political arrangement or a culture that freezes the nexus or is biased too heavily towards the public will be detrimental to the kind of growth of personality that many assume privacy-based societies such as ours are designed to promote.[1]

A hypothesis worth considering is that a media-filled public space usurps functions that should be part of the individual's own hard and long apprenticeship with life. It puts externalities, outward appearances, in the way of an inner development. It prevents the kind of coming to terms with life that once took from tradesmen a fair portion of a lifetime but earned them a place of respect in society. This is not the place to attempt a vindication of any such hypothesis, or to rehearse others' vindications of this or similar theories. But we may offer some of the terms in which it, or something close to its critical spirit, might be defended.

Take first the notion of space itself as a window in which players can be put on display. In the days of classic Hollywood films this space was limited. Too many players would cheapen the 'star value' of each. The movie moguls were therefore careful not to market too many personalities at a time.[2] In today's world of mass visual communication, especially television with its multiple audiences, the space is almost limitless. Stars designed to appeal to these audiences are constantly in demand, and the slots they fill, once they or their audiences fade, are constantly refilled by new 'personalities'. Simply proving one's talent has never been enough to secure the opportunity to appear on stage; today one fears it may seldom even be necessary. Talent-spotters with an eye to what can be dressed up in the way required will make sure the supply is kept up, so that the audience can be kept in place and the wheels of the entertainment industry greased and rolling.

If the expansion of the space might be thought to work to the democratic advantage of the gifted, allowing more of them to display their talent, the recording industry in fact works in the opposite direction. Like its Hollywood forebears, it finds that the fewer the names the audiences can aggregate themselves behind, the greater the overall aggregate. And it doesn't help the aspiring player that, for perhaps not altogether inscrutable reasons, the public shows a strong loyalty to the (in some branches not too long) dead. This might be looked on as a form of editorial processing ensuring a certain quality, but it is clearly very different from the kinds of restrictions placed on use of this public space when it was confined to the written word and the few outlets available to popular journalism. Those restrictions would in most cases also be self-imposed. For people using that space, to appear in it was something like taking a weekend stroll in public. One put on one's Sunday best: what was offered to the reading public had to be well written and worth reading. It being otherwise would reflect back both on authors and editors. Office doors could be knocked on and persons found inside who were accountable for what was published. If that is still true of the writing profession in spite of the infinite expansion of the space, the offerings of the media in general reflect more on what market surveys predict that audiences will want than on what a self-cultivated talent can provide. As for the Internet, among the many functions of the Super Information Highway is its provision of unlimited space for unedited advertisement and self-expression. The fact that it relieves players of the need to expose their performances and products to any processes of editorial selection, freeing the public player from restrictions that can also work unfairly, allows one to claim that the Internet serves an undeniably democratic purpose.[3] But the sheer volume of unscreened material that it makes available, as well as the fact that finding anything of value or interest becomes a matter of chance, means that the information seeker is made to resemble the poor scraping for items of value in a mountain of refuse.

Sure enough, the information supplied to our screens via news agencies and broadcasting companies is edited. It is very carefully edited, but the content and style of these cutely framed reports are dictated by a market-driven need to monopolize as much of the available audience (or space) as possible. The press maintains an expert balance between easily digested stereotype and attention-attracting novelty and crisis. It does so in order to sell itself, as well as for the journalists themselves to make careers, perhaps finally earning their own television talk shows. The talk shows themselves typically exploit bare items of current gossip, or recently acquired common knowledge, to make jokes at the expense of public figures, and for celebrities – exploiting just another form of publicity – to reveal yet another mask, a friendly and approachable one, under the thinly veiled pretence that it is the real selves behind the public masks they are revealing. The host quips, the studio audience whistles and laughs on cue and a worldwide television audience joins in.

Exaggeration? Certainly. If this consistently negative view of things is not supplemented by an account of the excellence and indispensability of much journalism and undoubted advantages offered by the Internet, it must itself be labelled a stereotype. Criticism of the media is a common enough occupation. Some may take it to indicate that matters are under control. But in the media themselves, on which most of us depend for our information about events 'out there', such criticism simply tends to become yet another event to be delivered to a captive audience.

Where else then can it be voiced? Frequently, the motivation conveyed to the public for such criticism, sometimes even promoted as a form of self-criticism, though only because the critic is a member of the same lodge, so to speak, is the desire to protect privacy. In our society that is just the sort of thing we would speak out for. But how widely the private freedom that the media are nowadays attacked for invading differs from the freedoms the press once campaigned to make possible by fighting for its own freedom. That freedom was defended as a bulwark against a corrupt or repressive power, an ideal that fortunately survives in investigative journalism. Today, when we criticize the press for invasions of privacy, the criticism itself is reported in the press and offered to the reader as an opportunity for *schadenfreude*, which then attracts its own audience. Discomfiture among the celebrated has always been a popular source of entertainment, but never more so than today. We need celebrity in others, and not having it ourselves, we like to see those who do have it in difficulties. Whether envy or a scorn typical of a consciously non-deferential society, these are not fine feelings, and disrespect easily becomes a way of life.

There is nothing new in the claim that the media lift us out of the real world into a world of easily digested stereotypes. But the extent of the removal is perhaps not fully appreciated. Instead of locating us where the action is, the media leave us with no real sense of location at all. Not having it we are unable to share in what we are shown. As the television camera closes slowly in on the stony face about to break down in grief and dwells there until it does so, we are brought no closer to grief itself. When the face crumbles and the tears appear in close up we either think, 'I can't stand it' and turn to another channel, or merely note once again that much is wrong with the world and wait for the more cheerful item bound to follow. That this conforms with our hypothesis that a media-filled public space puts outward appearances in the way of an inner development is easy to see. No genuine feelings are evoked or can be cultivated by brief cuts showing the reactions of strangers in conditions of misery. At most one can either gaze in helpless fascination or relive the professional distance of the cameraman taking the shots. If the two are combined we are not far from the peculiar fascination of pornography.

The same desensitization, or emotional pacification, of the observer is brought about by the constant repetition that is a feature of televisual imagery. What was real and made our hearts jump becomes mere illustration. That first sight of two large passenger jets plunging into each of the Twin Towers left an indelible image. Especially the second, since then it was clear there was no mistake. If incredulity was the first reaction, on the part both of eyewitnesses and of television viewers, subsequent images invoked horror rather than disbelief. We saw people, not just bodies, falling from their office windows and pedestrians fleeing clouds of dust as the metal frames melted under a heat they were not designed to resist. The images haunt us even now, when the initial horror is less easy to recapture. Yet, today that image of the jets is a standard 'visual aid' to almost any television mention of 11 September, just as close-ups of a syringe penetrating an arm accompany almost any reporting of matters medical. But what is now a movie sequence, from which the horror is erased, belongs to a train of events that of this date still produces its horrific images, among them that of a wired-up and hooded prisoner. That particular image now serves, too, as a regular background to discussions of atrocities on Iraqi detainees perpetrated by the US military. The sense of outrage may linger for a long time, and through public opinion it has its remedial effects, but the image itself is already just part of the television journalist's stock in trade. No doubt it will soon appear in glossy collections as well as in history books to come.

But if a tendency in the expansion of public space, noted here, is to discourage and even exclude active participation, the same public space is also one into which people can actually vanish. How so? Isn't the great 'out there' just where we can at last escape anonymity, be someone, even make some lasting mark on the world, speak and listen to each other?

That we can, literally speaking, merge with a crowd is obvious enough. We can escape notice by doing that, whatever the reasons. Where someone is being openly persecuted, you may merge with the crowd in order not to suffer the same treatment. In a more abstract sense you can do the same by not coming out and defending someone in public. You may, out of envy perhaps, hold back your praise of someone. You may even merge with the crowd when you agree with it, for instance letting the crowd's criticism do for your own or in general when you want to support a view but hold your support of it secret. In a society as privacy-based as ours the best way in *public* to avoid threats to privacy will always be to merge with the public, to toe the line, to be invisible in thought and habit – whether this means dressing and thinking in office grey or adopting some garish trend in some circles where office grey would be conspicuously out of place.

However, there is also a sense in which it is *oneself* that gets lost in the crowd. The above examples may even be seen as cases in point. One way of losing yourself in the crowd is to be so infected by its opinions as to come to hold them in respect of an opinion you would not have held had you not joined the crowd, and which, freeing yourself from the crowd, you come to realize was a foolish opinion. Something like this seems to happen in late-night television talk shows. In responding in unison, whether spontaneously or on cue, to the host, the individuals who elect or are chosen to form the studio audience cease to behave as individuals. In becoming the obedient audience of an expert nudge-and-wink artist, they merge with each other in a way that their numbers and composition make no difference. You may count them if you want, or the ticket office can do that. But the count doesn't mean anything since in fact no 'one' is there. Even if a countable number of seats are filled, the private citizens who found their way to the studio have vanished, along with their individualities, into this audience. As for those artists themselves, the talk-show hosts, they are not really there either, hiding as they do behind carefully constructed exteriors. But the more significant aspect of the talk show is the opportunity it provides for the expression of opinions without being personally accountable for them. It offers a perfect setting for someone wishing to invoke popular opinions, attitudes, or prejudices without taking personal responsibility for them. After all, it is only entertainment. It is as such that the talk show also provides a safe venue for the vulgar put-down.

As illustrations of the negative nature of the influence of the media on personal development, these analogies may seem too special for the purpose. It can also be objected that they are over-described: people surely retain their identities when they become members of audiences, even of studio audiences that laugh or applaud on cue; while, to their audiences before the television and in the studio alike, the talk-show hosts are, and know they are, just one among many means of diversion available to a modern public.

Let both points stand. What the cases illustrate, whether the reader agrees or disagrees that they also exemplify them, are ways in which, in the generation of what is called public opinion, the expansion of public space through the media discourages personal engagement. It does so almost to the same extent that it encourages mental passivity. Two negative consequences are, first, opinion is generated by forces beyond the individual's control, and second, the individual is denied a process of self-learning and inner development. The two latter are conditions of the ability to ascend to a level of judgement of the kind that Hume called 'general opinion'.

As for public opinion, it was hinted that this notion, like that of the public as a body, is used almost exclusively by journalists or their readers, among these of course also politicians sensitive to public support. 'Public opinion' easily conjures up images of groups of people murmuring, shaking their heads, and occasionally frowning in the direction of the government. It is more realistically cashed out into notions of individuals separately or in small groups, very occasionally or over longer periods and in somewhat half-hearted ways, forming decisions about how to vote at the next election – or more urgently but seldom, about whether to demonstrate or even join or, if authorized, call a strike. Probably only then is there any calculation, in the public itself and the press (with assistance from the media's statisticians), as to how many share a certain salient view. Frequently the basis, if any, in a population for claims made by interviewers who begin with expressions like 'people are saying . . .', or 'there is a general feeling that . . .', 'what of the suspicion that . . .?', etc. is owing to what journalists themselves have already attributed in print to 'the public'. Their audience is composed of individual readers, who then 'disappear' individually into an anonymous acceptance of what they have read. In a world where journalism commands so much attention, more often than not what is called public opinion is a product of what journalists themselves say to one another when they meet at the bar.

Well, why not? Aren't they, too, members of the public? Indeed, being such well-informed, especially privileged members, is it not right in a way that we should regard the press as the public's mouthpiece? Not in the sense that whatever it says on its own account, signed as it were in its own name, can be said to represent the public's opinion. The reason is that the opinions propagated in the press, whether anonymously or signed by respected journalists, are just as much responsible for forming those audiences that acquiesce in such published opinions, and by the same token for forming the public that acquires them, as they are reflections of what individuals in any large portion of the population think.

# Seven

In April 2003, several US soldiers died in a helicopter crash on the east coast of the United States. The President and the press called them heroes and they were given the burial with full military honours which that status requires. Why, you might ask, when US soldiers die in what, from a journalistic point of view, are high enough numbers but before seeing combat, are they described as heroes? It sounds as though new meaning were being given to the phrase 'jumping the gun'. In connection with that you might ask why the suicidal acts of desperate young men and women elsewhere, with no army to defend them, not only cannot qualify them for that status, but instead earn them the vilifying label of 'terrorists'. It may also occur to you that if nations with armies choose to perform acts of personal vengeance in the name of the nation, the guaranteed collateral damage that is always taken into the reckoning makes that choice already – except under the anti-quated rites and jargon of warfare – tantamount to premeditated murder. Should not sound common sense tell us that the helicopter crash prevented potential accomplices to murder being party to crime?

But whose common sense? Isn't it a truism that what strikes some people as common sense others see, equally common-sensically in their eyes, to be tainted with prejudice, rhetoric, or 'spin'? How can we be sure the revised readings suggested here are nearer the truth? What is common sense to one person is not common sense to another.

A case may be made for a common sense nevertheless, properly so-called, a vantage point from which alternative descriptions and evaluations to those just cited come into view. To a large extent, habits and rites of praise and blame, habits and rites reinforced in the public by governmental rhetoric and the media, may be seen for what they are. The jargon can be uncovered for what it is and euphemisms and the opposite replaced by a more literal truth.

But then again, what is to count as literal truth? Are not all descriptions to some extent readings and replaceable? No doubt. The case for a common sense will be more compelling if defended on behalf of an ability not so much to arrive at truth as to form a certain kind of critical judgement. Earlier we distinguished two notions: a general opinion as the product of a state of mind congenial to making judgements, and public opinion as a disposition to feel strongly about some topic that is brought to attention in the public sphere. The common sense we need is to be identified more closely with the former. In making a case for a common sense, we would therefore be joining forces with Hume in his appeal to general opinion, something in respect of which as, quoted earlier, 'in all questions with regard to morals, as well as criticism there is no other standard by which any controversy can be decided'.[1] The proposal would be that a critical common sense does enable us to distinguish between less and more distorted versions of what happens in the world.

What is this vantage point, how does one arrive at it, and how would you know that you have done so? There is no easy answer, but if it is true that there are standards of judgement more or less integral to the way we perceive our society, in the way suggested by Taylor's discussion of social imaginaries, referred to earlier,[2] then one answer to what the vantage point is would be that it is a position, within the society, from which its view of itself has become explicit. As for arriving at that position, perhaps no one can. It is not that panoptical vision notoriously leaves out the point of view of the viewer; on the contrary, the danger in this case is that the point of view of the viewer is necessarily partial and obscures what would seem evident from the points of view of others. For instance, the verdicts on the illustrations given here may be revisable in the light of views from somewhere else. The only test may be that of time. We must wait and see what judgements claiming to state more literal truths catch the imaginations of many people.

A more difficult problem is the practical one of getting a hearing for such judgements. By definition almost, the more literal truths are not in great demand, since if they were, there would be a tendency for opinion to converge on them. The problem is that, as we noted earlier, public opinion resembles far less what you would expect of an appeal to Humean general opinion than it does those potentially disruptive tides and currents of popular mood. Today the factions Hume feared have been largely domesticated in the form of party politics, replaced by what is now universally referred to as 'terror', a theme we will return to. As for the divided opinions that are now typically represented in differences of party programme, we may note how often the way public opinion behaves is described in the press in terms of 'surges', for instance of support for the President or the Prime Minister, which can then 'subside', of 'currents' of opinion and 'waves' of popular feeling.

The reasons for this are many. Part of it must be the fact that public opinion is a response to often unpredicted historical events. The public (meaning any number of us) is usually taken by surprise, or its interest in and attention to looming crisis become undivided only slowly. Lippmann crisply remarks, 'The public will arrive in the middle of the third act and will leave before the last curtain, having stayed just long enough perhaps to decide who is the hero and who the villain of the piece'.[3] The fairly regular rhythms of political life also play their part. There is, for instance, a concentration of appeals to the public at times of election, but a later falling off as things either arrive at or revert to a status quo that only the opposition will feel occupationally bound to try to disturb. The degree of credit an elected leader initially acquires also diminishes but does so more gradually, though its demise may be hastened by whatever truth there is to Addison's adage that the public is quicker to censure than to praise. If true, one suspects the adage too is no simple truth. Envy, boredom, seeing through the glitter of the wrapping, evident failure to fulfil promises (for protection, abundance, etc.), all these very different factors may contribute. But serious censure tends to arise only when events of certain kinds are widely publicized, events offending some quite deeply embedded sensibility, for instance, a revulsion at injustice.

Of many examples, the Rodney King case in Los Angeles in 1992 is fairly typical. This involved the beating up of a black man by four white police officers, who were charged with assault but acquitted, and where the beating was recorded on film. Riots ensued, which only subsided when two of the officers were later sentenced. Other cases may have less visible flashpoints so that what a wider audience first sees is the conflagration itself, as in the six days of the Watts riot in Los

Angeles in 1965, which erupted after the routine arrest of a drunk driver. Instead of tides and currents we might talk here of disturbances due to features of the seabed causing ripples and even larger manifestations on the surface. Stable preferences become visible as 'waves' when people are roused from their civil slumbers by deeply threatening events. Even where the instances are not physically close to home they can bring to mind the everyday possibility of the same occurring locally. Governments are then forced to respond not just because riots are an inconvenience and can spread, but because the injustice has been brought to the notice of a world whose respect and support they are forced to retain. Survival in modern politics often depends on preserving a humane image on the world stage, a fact of some significance.

Suppose there were only one nation, a global state. We have recently become very aware that censure can take the other direction, directed at dissenters rather than leaders. This happens typically in times of national crisis, real or unreal. Here another stable popular preference surfaces, this time in favour of government policy and the leadership. Subjected to 'terror' from an 'axis of evil', for example, in its anxiety a nation will close round even a weakly supported national leader. Censure on the part of the public now becomes a form of treason and those who dare to oppose whatever the government decides, or even raise questions about it, are branded as traitors. True, there can be revulsion at such a turn. Reasonable people will react at the anomaly of their nation, dedicated as it is to freedom, having its citizens arrested for wearing T-shirts emblazoned 'peace too is patriotic'. The existence of an American concentration camp at Guantanamo Bay and plans to try captives and construct a death chamber there for the execution of what most consider at best prisoners of war (captured, after all, in what is billed by the leadership as a *war* on terrorism), all this can easily stir up a 'wave' of revulsion not unlike the one Voltaire set in motion by informing Europe of cases like that of Jean Calas. Nevertheless, and to pursue the oceanographic metaphor further, in home waters and times of national crisis the force of such waves is broken by the built-in credit accruing in the popular mind to the leadership. Such bias (due as much, understandably, to wishful thinking as to habits of loyalty) is often compounded by an ignorance, wilful among the public, deliberately instilled within the state, and typically spread by inherited distortions of history and tradition.

In order to acquire sufficient force in circumstances like these, the waves in question must become phases in a groundswell that carries over to other parts of the world, to areas unaffected by this particular bias, where the undesirable effects of short-sighted international policies and incipient imperialism on the part of one nation can be hindered by popular opinion in others. One powerful argument against political globalization, then, is the need to retain an effectively censorious public, one that must be wider than that of a single state.

It would be wrong, however, to think of the pressure as exclusively top-down. As mentioned earlier, a common tendency within a population is to acquiesce in a government's policies of non-involvement, typically from fear of upsetting internal stability. But people may also be roused to deplore what they see as a weak-kneed passivity inconsistent with their own and the nation's tough image, thus threatening to undermine their own and the nation's reputation. Examples abound here too. It is generally accepted, for instance, that it was only in the face of a general restlessness on this count at home, and of pressure from the French president, that President Clinton began the bombing of Serbia.[4] Yet a popular memory, selective in itself and suitably aided by the press, is more than willing to repair such damage. The American public may now look back on the Serbian adventure as proof of a determination to eradicate 'evil' wherever it is found. We forget that, as proof that a US-led 'war' on terror was not a war on Islam, a succeeding president exploited in the guise of a 'defence of Muslims' what was in effect a last-minute decision made under popular pressure.

It may be unfortunate that due to its singular influence in the world today the US should provide so many vivid illustrations of the vagaries and weaknesses of this 'thing' called public opinion. But the fact of their appearing, especially to outsiders, so painfully evident in that context reveals something of the consequences of having to maintain a nation or commonwealth as 'extensive' as the US. More than most, it is a nation that sustains itself on its image and historical record, in both of which it makes a heavy investment. Who, for example, on visiting the Holocaust museum in Washington could assume anything but that the US has a record of hands-on opposition to known genocide abroad?

In cases like this the literal truth is too easy to discover for us to have to talk about a privileged vantage point from which to discern it. And that is the way it is in general. The vantage point is reached by moving not closer to the truth but further away. The evidence is already available but it requires a certain kind of disengagement even to want to examine it. One must first be willing to envisage alternatives to the view on show. We may expect this more readily of an outsider, but then if the outsider in one context is an insider in another, there is a danger of demonization. The more reliable outsiders are those who acquire some distance to their own political settings. That can be either in the present or as a member of a later public able, due to distance in time, to loosen its loyalties to what is past. Critical outsidership in the present is something we shall return to, but one quite significant factor here is the familiar reticence we feel compelled to maintain due to fear that in admitting the truth we are playing into the hands of our nation's enemies, who will again distort the truth but this time in the service of an unfriendly stereotype. A glaring example is the widespread refusal in Germany today, even among intellectuals, openly to support the Palestinian cause. The fear, which on any plausible account of what it is to employ one's reason is an irrational fear though unfortunately no less real for that, is that by doing so they will be accused of anti-Semitism.

On the face of it, such lack of good sense appears too absurd for the explanation to be a simple one. However there are several things one can point to in mitigation of accusations of unreason here, including the point just made that in making the rational point one may be playing into the hands of those less rational. But in the remainder of this chapter, two quite different perspectives will be outlined, each with its characteristic perspective on unreason and how to escape it.

The former is a philosophical perspective. By that I mean a perspective that appeals to what everyone in a properly rational mood would be expected to assent to. It differs from Hume's general opinion in, at least on my reading of Hume, supposing a specifically philosophical vantage point above the variety of traditions.[5] It may be illustrated by a now familiar example of a well-known philosopher's encounter with what, for want of a better name, may be called public unreason. It is worth examining the implications of the example in some detail. It relates to Peter Singer's cancelled lecture tour in Germany in 1989. Singer had been billed in June 1989 to give a public lecture, in the university town of Marburg, on euthanasia. His general thesis was to be (cautiously enough) that, in certain circumstances, it might be 'ethically permissible to take active steps to end the lives of infants'. The circumstances in question included severe disability where death is considered to be best for the infant, but also in some cases where consideration can be taken of the family as a whole (for example where there is no acceptable alternative to the child staying with the family).[6] The lecture was to be part of a symposium entitled 'Bioengineering, Ethics and Mental Disability' under the auspices of two large organizations for parents of intellectually disabled infants. However, these organizations were put under pressure to cancel their invitation to Singer, on the grounds that although his views might be discussed in closed academic circles, he should not be allowed to promote them in public.

The point made by those opposing the debate was that, although in the interests of freedom of speech it should be allowed to go ahead in spite of their distaste for the topic, it was one that should be aired behind closed doors and according to the special conventions of philosophical debate. There are several reasons in favour of such a forum. The conditions there are of a kind in which opposition can be effectively made, something that may easily not be the case when opposition is in the hands of people unschooled in debate. There is also that matter of disengagement. In academic circles, the way you address a topic matters as much as, if indeed not more than, the topic itself or indeed the outcome. In light of such factors such a discussion need not provoke any serious harm.

What harm? For those who opposed the position in principle it would be the position's actually coming to be accepted. They might harbour deep scruples about taking life in general, or more strategically, see this as the thin end of a wedge that could end in old-fashioned eugenics. Others might cite a quite different danger: the position being accepted under the persuasive influence of an apparently rational discussion but in which the idea of rationality and the rules of debate associated with it gave Singer an unfair advantage. The fear would be that other sources of insight relevant to such an important issue would have no chance to take effect, a chance which in the interests of truth they should be given. We will return to this.

Singer sees it in another light. The harm he found himself forced to consider was one he believed he should not really have to consider. It was what some (or enough) people thought might all too easily arise just from him presenting his thesis, even though it was the cautious one mentioned. Simply proposing it might refresh grim memories of the consequences of the Nazi euthanasia programme and could even be exploited, if not intended, as an attempt to steer people's minds back in the same direction. It was in fact the public identification of Singer's philosophically argued conclusion with Nazi malpractices in the recent past that brought about the widespread demand that the invitation be cancelled. The case is similar to that in which pro-Palestinian sentiments are taken to be expressions of anti-Semitism. The explanation lies in Germany itself, due to the not-so-distant Nazi past, in a sensitivity that inclines people prejudicially to attribute views like Singer's to a mentality of the Nazi cast.

There are two sharply diverging ways of looking at this. According to one it demonstrates the continuing hold of

intolerance and a narrow-minded refusal to foster free intellectual inquiry. As a philosopher, Singer not unsurprisingly
sees it in this light. Characteristically he also draws from the
local explanation a wider conclusion about bio-ethical
inquiry in general. 'Bio-ethics', he affirms, 'is a discipline that
leads to the questioning of values and ethical doctrines . . .
previously . . . treated as sacrosanct.' These doctrines he takes
to be linked closely to religious beliefs. Intolerance of free
discussion has moreover a broad political basis which permits
more subtle ways of preventing the spread of free bio-ethical
discussion, for example restrictions on funding. Singer
concludes:

> There is a clear need to develop a broader appreciation of the
> importance of an atmosphere of support for rational
> discussion of controversial ideas, in bioethics and
> elsewhere. One step towards doing this would be an
> institutional means – such as an international association of
> bioethics – which could show the united support of
> bioethicists from all over the world, whatever their views, for
> the right to discuss freely issues in bioethics.[7]

It is interesting that while Singer's opponents linked his
position with Hitler's Germany, he linked them with Ayatollah
Khomeini, tarring them with the brush of religious funda-
mentalism. It is important that the bio-ethicist is a philosopher, not a practitioner, that is, not a physician or surgeon,
a professional facing daily the problems bio-ethicists discuss.
Bio-ethics, like other areas of applied philosophy, business
ethics for instance, employs traditional methods of reasoning
to tackle ethical dilemmas of professional and political life. It
draws on an armoury of methods established by philosophy's
recent analytic past and on standard versions of the more

enduring moral theories. Bio-ethics has in this way contributed to a public image of the philosopher as a professional among others, and of philosophy itself as a service industry dispensing universally applicable guidelines for ethically acceptable behaviour. Singer's way of seeing the situation fits exactly this pattern. It calls for employment of the cool light of objective reason and seeks an international forum for the debate free from contextual interference. The perspective here is one we find also in proposals to define truth in terms of consensus. In political life that is an impossibility: disagreement is the name of the political game and universal agreement here is inconceivable. Even the attempt by philosophers to formulate procedures that maximize the possibility of agreement seem misconceived if they imply that truth is a light that will shine once all in which we disagree has been discarded as due either to lack of relevant information or else 'darkness'. There is the idea that, given the impossibility of a universal debate, the task of arriving at what is virtual agreement can be entrusted to certain arrangements designed to ensure that the results of actual debates, in which comparatively few directly engage, conform with that to which free and equal citizens *could* reasonably agree. This idea, implicit in Habermas's notion of an ideal speech situation, designed precisely to aim at such a consensus, sounds excellently democratic. But it is an abstracting idea that ignores the reality of politics and is for that reason not at all democratic.

There is, however, an alternative perspective: one from which the opposition Singer encountered appears as something to which he himself contributed. The resistance that the generalizing philosopher meets can be due simply to fear, perhaps a double fear: fear of the return of a very real past that the topic itself as well as the thesis would arouse, combined with a fear that yet another order was being imposed on the public, this time by a regime whose edicts are hammered out on the anvil of a reason impervious to recent history and local feelings.

Directing an appeal of this kind, and in such a way, to people with complicated attitudes bound up with their history can itself appear profoundly irrational. It is to ask people to revise their opinions but taking no account of the nature of the opinions themselves or of what it is that evokes and sustains them. The travelling rationalist who must regard local variation as irrelevant and 'dark' is a development of what began in the attempt to protect informed debate from the disruptive influence of unschooled popular opinion. But in a society where education is virtually universal, popular opinion can no longer be described as unschooled; what we have now is a form of irrationality not of ignorance. The alternative perspective, then, is one that adopts a common sense that sees irrationalities for what they are and is able to judge the morality of a society that fails to divest itself of them or to develop from within these irrationalities. The disengagement that an ability to see a cultural community's moral shortcomings requires is not a disinterested disengagement of the kind that Dreyfus criticizes in a companion work in this series. That would mean failing to appreciate the nature of the forces at work in the shaping of opinion. From this other perspective the forces may not appear so dark, and some may even appear beneficial. With its collective gut feeling, the public may act as a brake on what it senses – at times, it may prove, wisely – to be facile proposals for innovation or short-term measures designed to bring instant credit to career-minded politicians or the premature application of the findings of over-enthusiastic scientists.

European resistance to gene-manipulated food may be due not just to a mindless reliance on nature; it may be traced to a healthy decline in a once over-confident trust in science in general.[8] Similarly in medical ethics. Popular prejudice against surrogate motherhood and artificial insemination can be argued against by pointing out the advantages, for instance for infertile couples, cementing marriages in this way, and so forth. Popular 'prejudice', unschooled in philosophical forensics, might defend itself not by argument but by resorting to vivid turns of phrase which put the matter in bold relief, for instance by referring, as has been done, to 'shop-floor motherhood', a metaphor specifically designed like 'Frankenfoods' to present the innovation in a bad light, but which 'progressive' thinkers will object to as 'darkly' tendentious and intellectually reprehensible.

The common sense we are seeking is first of all that of an individual. It is possible from that always tenable 'outsider' position which modern society provides for its public. Anyone in the aggregate public of a modern state can turn reflectively away from immersion in current world-engagement to see this engagement in a wider light. Any individual can rise above the fog that blinds moral vision when fear of losing what it has gained in its privacy is the primary political concern. To see that the public domain has been turned into a sector that matters only when it fails to deliver protection, to realize the extent to which governments see their duties (easily advertised by them to voters as protecting their private worlds) mainly in terms of the economic survival of the nation, to realize how this in turn calls for its continual growth on a limited planet, and to realize that other societies frown on the infinite economic exploitation of a finite world, and that well over half of the world's population disapprove of the use of this world as a playground for protected privacies, whether by tourists, tuned-in teenagers, or media magnates, or even politicians with personal grudges – all this can and has to be laid on the shoulders of the individual. There is no other valid perspective.

By that, I of course do not mean that the world will be saved by individuals rather than groups, by single initiatives rather than by concerted action, of whatever kind. The point is an epistemological one. It is about our sources of understanding, of the depths of our individual vision, of how we can help each other to wider and deeper understanding, and work our way through what come to appear obvious distortions so as to approach something that could be called a common sense. Nor, of course, do I mean that approaching such a sense is achieved in a state of unworldly solipsism; it arises in the company one keeps and the experience one accumulates. But it also requires an ability to resist lazy habits and rise above them and to digest and re-digest one's experience, and to have an open eye for the kind of company one keeps.

The historian Thucydides tells how the Athenians came to re-elect his contemporary, Pericles, as their leader in spite of their fury at his having allowed their land to be ravaged by the Peloponnesians. He writes that although 'as a community' their leader's eloquence succeeded in assuaging their anger, nevertheless 'as private individuals' they still smarted under their losses and sufferings. It was only after he had been fined that 'public feeling' against him subsided. And then, quite soon, 'according to the way of the multitude, they elected him again as general and committed all their affairs into his hands, having become less sensitive to their private and domestic afflictions, and understanding that he was the best man of all for the public necessities'.[9]

It is only natural, when danger threatens, to place public security before private redress. In our times, the dangers are harder to pin down than for the hard-tried Athenians. They knew who the enemy was and, in the light of no obvious alternative, the decision to retain Pericles was reasonable. Our own enemies face us on the pages of newspapers and in the official mouthpieces of our leaders. By then, they tend to be monsters of image-management and the leaders who take it upon themselves to defend us against them hardly less so. Occupied as we generally are with our own matters, and 'according to the way of the multitude', we ourselves naturally tend to accept what we see and hear. We merge with the multitude, not wanting to realize how little its opinions are its and ours our own.

The common sense we need is one that allows truths to appear that, prior to attaining its vantage point, we may not have liked. Among these can be the realization that the forces threatening us are partly generated by our own society. The darkness we see abroad, and when at home as something foreign, and which we oppose to our own light, may be an illusion due to blindness to the effects of the aggressive and also destructive nature of our own way of life. We may come to realize that living in a world of protected privacy is to live in a state of constant fear, a fear that includes the fear of showing or even feeling it. To common sense, what we call 'dark' and even 'evil' may appear less alien to anything we can imagine ourselves ever considering or condoning. Common sense is not conciliation or negotiation or compromise; it is a better sense of difference that can alleviate the pressures that these merely presuppose. It may allow us to look with under-standing on the desperate acts of those in other cultures who feel at the mercy of the blind forces driving our own. We may even end up acknowledging their desperation and fear, even grasping why tourist destinations, discothèques in Muslim lands and sky-scraping – or heaven-storming – centres of world trade should be their preferred targets.

If situations like Voltaire's were repeated and an audience created for a shared vision along these lines, that would go some way to vindicating the claim that the sense it gives to us of things is a 'common' sense. The more common it is the better able to prevent politicians relying on self-servingly short memories. It will be less certain that 'in a month or a year events will have moved along'. 'The tyrant had to go' will cause fewer heads to nod, knowingly but mindlessly, when uttered, as so often and with such finality, as an argument-stopping excuse for what it cost in human terms to remove him.

# Eight

So far, with regard to the public, what it means to us today is little more than a catalogue of names – a list, merely, of those who, according to their various backgrounds, sensibilities, etc., may come to form more or less ephemeral aggregates around some shared focus of concern. These can be of many kinds, communal as well as more or less political. It seems to be a feature of modern society indeed to develop communal activities, locally or in groups, that for their participants have far greater significance for their lives than any political engagement. These projects exist at all levels from local fan clubs to organized pilgrimages,[1] from Gardener of the Year to World Idol contests. The concerns they aggregate around can have a political flavour when politically sensitive events are conveyed to a sizeable enough audience. The church, in all its forms, represents another concerted communal activity that partly protects itself from political engagement, but addresses politics on certain salient issues, and can in some countries, as for instance in South America, be enduringly engaged in political struggle. The thought was also that popular attention is something governments employ the considerable means at their disposal in order, as the case may be, either to exploit or foreclose. But beyond this propensity to be roused from its private preoccupations when touched at sore points by the media, we have found little positive to say of the public itself. The most said is that it is composed of citizens exploiting their legally protected private rights to build and furnish their privacy.

Many will say this is an inaccurate account. After all, thanks to modern communication, today's public is 'in' on most of what happens, at least on the political surface, which is where the kind of 'crunch' that concerns it eventually comes. Moreover, and this is a significant factor, regarding the processes or procedures that lead to major political decisions there is still some feeling at large that these decisions are made under its surveillance, a kind of guarantee that it exercises some kind of constant control, or even that in some indirect way there is public agreement with what governments decide and then do. As in ancient Rome, just by being in close touch with the dealings of senators and magistrates, those who met to exchange views in the forum were made to feel that their opinions were acknowledged and somehow mattered, so too the publicity that surrounds modern politicians conveys a general impression that, being similarly forged 'under the public eye', their decisions are products of a popular feedback. Since criticism is routinely expected from the side of the opposition, governments themselves may feel encouraged to assume that, if only public censure does not exceed expected limits, they can take the continuing support of a 'silent majority' for granted. A public with its sensory apparatus constantly keyed to a communications network that relays policy decisions against their daily backgrounds may for that reason feel satisfied that it has the 'ear' of an audience-sensitive government.

There are other reasons too why the public may feel content with only limited 'hands-on' engagement in political decision-making, or indeed for most of the time with none.

Given a contractual element in the way democratic societies understand themselves, once a government is 'in', it has an authority that only in very exceptional circumstances can be impeached. By voting it in, even that part of the public that voted for an alternative has consented to bow to a government's decisions. Admittedly, in liberal democracies this would not be used as an argument for withholding criticism and reminding the government of its electoral promises. A stronger excuse for giving the government its head is the idea that its decisions should stand in any case just because they are arrived at through procedures established to ensure as much consensus as possible. For the procedures do not have to be assumed to guarantee right decisions; on this procedural view the 'should' here is moral and so the decision should stand even if you think it wrong. Endorsement by the Security Council of a policy of military intervention in Iraq would override any political or even moral objections the individual might have had to such a policy. Similarly if instead of failing to reach a decision at all, the Council had endorsed a policy of non-intervention, ways other than military force would have to be proposed. Had the US or 'coalition' in those circumstances intervened anyway, this would have invoked moral revulsion among many. As it happened, in the moral vacuum left by the Security Council's failure to reach internal agreement, the US was able to adopt a superior moral stance and accuse the United Nations of vacillation and worse.

It is clear enough, however, that when invoked in this way, whether as a rhetorical weapon in the defence of political decisions or as justification by the individual for not forming his or her own judgement, morality itself assumes the guise of a mere pawn in a game. In one case the political interests of a nation or its leaders are pursued under simple-minded moral mottoes designed to appeal to an unthinking majority; in another individuals exploit a fairly sophisticated tradition of moral thinking to justify staying on the sidelines. In a post-Nietzschean age like ours it has become normal to interpret morality against a background of power relations or networks. For those inspired by Nietzsche himself, however, not only the characteristic puerility and at times patent hypocrisy of current political appeals to popular moral sense, but also the abject delegation of political and moral responsibility to formal procedures, must both betoken a situation in which morality itself is conspicuously absent. A morally sensitive public has little reason to be content with the manner or extent of its participation in political affairs. The degree to which the public is 'in' on these affairs falls far short of what theorists have required of popular consent.

A factor Lippmann failed to account for in stressing the distinction between outsiders and insiders is that errors of government are not merely failures of expertise but often lapses of common morality. That they are so is hidden usually by the sanctity of *realpolitik* as the framework within which politicians are 'forced' to operate. But the language used is often designed to appeal to an electorate not so constrained. In that case the moral terms in which the explanation is offered must to an outsider seem entirely specious. Here is an area where governments may cover up or try to explain away their errors but in respect of which, as insiders, they have no special expertise.

It nevertheless requires what in Lippmann's terms might be called an 'extended outsidership' to be in, or come into, a position where criticism of this kind can be mounted. The distance may be needed even for it to become evident that such pressure needs to be exerted. An 'extended outsider' is someone who is to a degree immune to the influence of powerful and centrally disseminated narratives of the kind issued by administrations especially in times of crisis, immune in a way that Lippmann's outsiders, being simply at the mercy of insiders, will tend not to be. For reasons not at all hard to understand, at times of national crisis the majority of citizens tend not to be immune.

The reasons are clear enough. A multicultural as well as geographically extended nation needs to feel secure in its government as the protector of its integrity. Not least is this true of a nation whose basic principle is that privacy above all be protected. The government in its turn, in order to protect its reputation and status in this respect, has to give the impression of being the strong guardian of the nation. It can do so, as mentioned earlier, through a loyal and centralized press corps disposed to provide a single story well suited to maintaining or restoring faith in the powers that be. In so far as they serve the principle of protected privacy in general, the public services, too, and the military are unifying factors, to say nothing of national sport. Heroic sporting achievements on behalf of the nation can be celebrated locally, thus connecting the periphery to the centre. The fact that fallen soldiers are buried with military honours in symbolically national ground softens the bitterness the bereaved may feel for their personal sacrifice, while any local resentment that remains will in any case be voiced at a convenient distance – something of which Hume would have recognized the significance.

Large commonwealths based on the protection of privacy are fragile. In one respect, the fragility is logical, simply because privacy is at risk once the system protecting it is under threat. To protect privacy you have to curtail it. It is often said that exposure to attack is a price that must be paid for freedom and that it is a price worth paying. Perhaps, but there is more to be said about freedom than that it is something worth paying that price for. The value of freedom must ultimately be judged by what freedom achieves. It is also true that in an important sense freedom, even when provided for, is something that itself still remains to be achieved. The public with its freedoms protected can be a willingly or wilfully manipulated public. It can be a public formed of individuals whose use of the freedom provided for falls short of the actions and attitudes the provision was designed to foster.

The fragility may be more than logical. The enterprises issuing from the privacies protected by the state can be read as vain attempts to obscure the more fundamental fragility of the human being itself. On this analysis, it is due to this that the privacy is exploited in the way so evident today in a consumerist society, exploited, that is, not to allow human beings to flourish in a community, but as an opportunity to ignore unacceptable truths about the human condition. A consistent application of the analysis might even take the communal activities in which people nevertheless engage on their own initiatives, of the kind just mentioned, as diversions designed to escape such truths.

At whatever level of analysis we begin or end, there is something sinister in the thought that a modern public may be impervious en masse to its shortcomings, and in its having an investment in remaining so.

Compare this situation with that of those 'replicants' in the classic movie *Blade Runner*. These knew their shortcomings and wanted to overcome them. In a run-down Los Angeles in 2019, these creatures of the high-tech Tyrell Corporation, not actually belonging to the world and with a four-year life span, return to their makers demanding an upgrading to full human status. Indeed, what these jumpy beings, who can turn up anywhere at any time, lack is everything human: inner lives, emotions, histories, roots. An ex-policeman, the eponymous blade runner, has the unenviable job of identifying these almost-humans and 'taking care of them'. One, Rachel, through a photo of what she takes to be her mother acquires a virtual memory of a past, a foot in the door so to speak. The blade runner falls for her.

An allegory, of course, and an exaggeration. But the reference to inner history and, if only implicitly, to a capacity to reflect and to develop powers of feeling and empathy, as well as to a sense of something missing, or in our context lost, speaks clearly enough to our theme. It does so in the general area of what is usually referred to as 'inner life'. That inner life is a feature of the individual. It can expand or it can fail to develop, and it can wither.

In philosophy, the individual has, for a long time, been discussed under the category of 'subject', typically the perceiving subject considered in opposition to, or 'over and against', the perceived 'object'. It is characteristic of much contemporary philosophy to play down the role of the subject, once the foundation of all philosophical reconstructions of knowledge. Descartes may well be, for all intents and purposes, dead as far as philosophy today is concerned, and very few will disagree with Habermas in his rejection of views in which the 'experiencing' subject remains 'the last court of appeal'.[2] Nevertheless, whatever justification there may be for rejecting it in certain areas traditionally central to philosophy, the idea of the experiencing subject as a final court of appeal need by no means be dead. It can even stand as a kind of target, not in the sense of something to hit and destroy, but as something to reach for for those who believe better justice can be done to the philosophy of the subject, particularly in terms of discernment, apprehension and, not least, self-awareness. Certainly, to dismiss the subject's role, even in Nietzsche, to 'the yes and no of the palate', as Habermas in one place does,[3] is to talk of the human subject as little more than a replicant.

The following comments are therefore offered by way of a proposal that this notion of a subjective court of appeal provides just the sound basis needed on which to resurrect the role of the subject and, with it, that central figure: the individual who is responsible for the politically influential opinions of 'the public'.

We may conveniently leave aside disputes about reason and its role and possible limitations. Or rather, we may let reason be just whatever you appeal to in support or criticism of a proffered position. There are innumerable positions or, when you accept them, standpoints. A standpoint is what you express when you say why you accept or reject a certain proposal, in our case a moral or a political proposal. There may be no clear line to be drawn between motivation and justification here, between what drives you to say something and reasons you may give for your view of the matter. But whatever people say expresses their view of where they stand, and the kinds of considerations that occur to them, there and then, in saying it. That this is reason enough is even more obvious where the views are backed by professional experience. Members of the medical and legal professions, as well as of various religious groups and sects, and committed non-believers, with or without professional 'philosophical' leanings, whether as utilitarians or deontologists or communitarians, are all more or less reliable purveyors of reasons.

To reserve the term 'reason' for those who think only abstractly would be tendentious in the extreme. One may be both a lawyer and an atheist, and even a philosopher, but it is as a lawyer that you know your way about the world.

On the other hand, the lawyer's vision qua lawyer is still only partial. And the same goes for all who know their way about in their professional domains. Is there no wider vision available?

In this age of the death of ideologies – 'grand narratives' – our social criticism tends not to be theoretical. That it is better not so was forcefully proclaimed in Karl Popper's *The Open Society and its Enemies* (1945). With his hard criticism of the belief in general laws of historical development, Popper's own proposal was that social reform should proceed by piecemeal social engineering. But following too slavishly the pattern of Popper's proposed piecemeal social engineering may be a mistake, strategically speaking. Perhaps even the very idea of a science of society is wrong at the outset. We may have to rise above the level of science or indeed of any of our professions, though without losing touch with what we learn there. A piecemeal approach can blind us to things that a broader perspective may bring to light, thus preventing insight into what is wrong and what is needed for change where change is possible.

'Seeing where things are going', talk of 'the tendency of the age', these imply a reflection, a position outside and possibly above the age. Not inconceivably such a reflection may be one that fails to reach up to the age, not seeing its good points but capable only of sour criticism ('youth no longer respects age', etc.). All too often critics of the present have compared their times with a golden past. Rejection of such criticism may, on the other hand, come from those with a utopian or at least romantic vision of the present as the threshold to a future defined abstractly in terms of freedom, authenticity, self-development, full use of human resources, etc. Existentialists, Beatniks, the Hippies and Youth Culture (in some of its aspects) have offered the promise of a way out of what is made to appear a cheaper form of life than the one(s) we are destined for. The conflict between environmentally concerned liberals and globalizing capitalists is a clash between diverging visions, each with its view of what promises to be a catastrophic outcome of not paying heed to their message: an impoverished nature or an unexploited richness – though the globalizers, too, promote their plan for the future as the only way of sustaining life on Earth, in their case in terms of increasing prosperity. We should accept that how one sees the age going (to the dogs or towards true freedom and self-fulfilment) may itself depend on cultural variables defining the forms reflection takes when it judges the age.

In the hands of philosophers such perspectival variables can survive simultaneously in the form of conflicting traditions of thought. Hubert Dreyfus's criticism of continuing strains of Enlightenment thought, targeting notably Habermas, is a case in point. Against Habermas's hopes for the public sphere as the space to recapture on behalf of political and moral virtue,[4] Dreyfus first levels objections that he sees anticipated in Kierkegaard's comments on the press, in particular the way in which a media-filled public sphere abstracts from the individual's world, thus depriving people of their footholds for individual initiative, while at the same time protecting them in the way we have noted from any sense of personal accountability. Where Habermas would regard these as difficulties to overcome, Dreyfus sees them as endemic to the public sphere itself and a basic fault in the

Enlightenment belief in a 'space in which the rational, disinterested reflection that should guide government and human life could be institutionalized and refined'.[5]

Whatever the philosophers say, is it not evident to everyone that a view of things wider than one's personal experience, professional or not, is generally available? By 'anyone' I am not referring to the anonymous public as such, a merely countable vote, for that is no one. I mean an individual with experience as a player and audience. Such experience can always be a vantage point from which to develop a reflective expertise that is at once synoptic and based directly on hands-on knowledge, quite unfiltered by some presupposed account of humankind, or of what is good in the long run for humanity.

Consider that lawyer. He or she is a member of the public, anonymous so far except as a listed name. But 'lawyer' narrows the field. So do many other labels and descriptions of the parts played in society by this member of the public. For the lawyer, legal experience is not the only horizon he or she works within, and even within that sphere many other horizons interact. As life goes on, with any quite ordinary powers of perspective, the horizon within which the lawyer's activities in that role operate can widen and extend to a world in which legal decisions also have their limits and where moral considerations intrude. The same is not only possible but likely for anyone in a position of responsibility, typically a position in 'public' service, though not necessarily in the pay of the state. As your reflective horizon expands, so does the range and depth of your sensibility, the force of concentrated intuition you are able to bring to bear on the actions and utterances of those in a position to influence your own actions. You are in a position to react tellingly to such actions and utterances as now visibly contravene deep-seated codes of behaviour accepted by the society you work in. But you may go further. You may learn to see the official versions of these codes themselves as but poor versions of codes even more deeply seated in the population and which you realize that you yourself share. Sharing them with others and observing the distance between them and the official moral jargon, you can be part of a wider vision, and in a position to let others share it. This is the degree, in the terms of Habermas's perhaps deliberately throwaway remark, to which a palate may be developed in its power of discrimination, in its sense of what to say 'yes' or 'no' to.

We gave examples earlier of revisions of standard perceptions of heroes and terrorists. In whatever way the events described by using these notions may be made to appear, it is open to any member of a society to sense, in the response to those events, the general tenor of that society's moral and political attitudes. The ability to see a cultural community's moral shortcomings requires a certain disengagement but, as we said earlier, not a disinterested disengagement of the sort that Dreyfus criticizes. What is needed is a distancing on the very basis of an engagement, from within it, and in extension of the expertise as it were, not in feigned ignorance of it. On the other hand, as with any personal narrative one may construct in a lifetime, it typically takes an outsider to note discrepancies between the narrative and the life itself. But then, as we have already noted, in modern western societies the outsider role, though it is typical as well as natural to try to escape from it, is one we are all inherently able to adopt. It is an uneasy position to hold, because from it everything you are and believe can be weighed in the balance. But that there is this resource from within is an avenue to salvation.

We need occasionally to step aside. Or meet in some public space where we are put in mind of how little of what we do or achieve counts, seeing things directly and without the interfering spins and refractions of the media or of their influence on our current perceptions. One such place is Ground Zero, where the Twin Towers once stood; these are to be replaced not only by a new tower, this time of Freedom, but also by something less rhetorical, a grove named 'reflecting absence'. It is not only a fitting symbol of the position from which reflection over the nature and setting for human fulfilment can take place; sight of the levelled terrain and memory of the terrible events that caused it can free the mind for a moment from its normally healthy addiction to the world, an addiction that easily creates enmity and division. It is a prospect that can produce a sense of human levelling. Kierkegaard said that coming to the point where all you can say positively of yourself is that you are a human being reveals the fundamental nullity of selfhood, the ultimate anonymity, a ground zero in which you stay put but at the same time move on, letting it educate your everyday. He predicted we would end up there and that it would be a good thing if we did.

Following Kierkegaard's diagnosis of his age as an age given to despair, we would have to see western culture as a massive cover-up operation, a way of diverting attention from this fundamental nullity by conceiving ourselves ever more creatively but desperately in worldly terms.

Whether Kierkegaard is right about despair being our basic trait – in his version it requires some correlative notion of faith – his belief that modern society drives us to a ground zero that we would rather not have to visit, is one that resonates today. Maybe we refuse at our peril to visit it. Building a tower to freedom is to avoid the issue of what freedom is and the duties it imposes. Whether or not the physical ground zero is rebuilt, the reflective possibility that it symbolizes is one we all carry with us.

It is wrong to cast privacy itself in the role of evil-doer. If privacy is bad by itself, it need not be so in itself. The confines of our protected privacies can be just what we need. True, 'privacy' conjures up notions of guardedness, selfishness and greed, even introversion and narcissism, not just intimacy and warmth. If asked what else is needed, a usual answer will be in terms of a concern for the interests of others. Philanthropy and public service are candidates, but the former is confined to the well-off and, regarding the latter, public-sector workers, however communally motivated, tend to be people like anyone else except for the fact that they perform overt social functions paid for by the state, not well paid as a rule, but with the security of a state pension.

Nevertheless, it does seem right to say that what is needed is to be found within the private sphere, and moreover at the level of the individual existence, of anonymity, and also that what is needed embraces a concern for the common good. In a society as expanded as ours, generating a sense of community requires a sense of acute common danger from outside: totalitarian leaders knew how to generate and preserve that sense. To bring off the connection between private and public in the way Hegel optimistically expected – with a society well conscious of its participation in the whole – may indeed require a totalitarian government. This would automatically spell the demise of 'the public' in the sense that Dewey, for instance, assumes, a public formed by individuals but also one whose demise was predictable for other reasons. The objection to applying anything like the Hegelian proposal today would be that it excluded the possibility we are pursuing, which assumes that the public is in place, an indeterminate aggregate that, until those forming it engage each others' attention in the player-audience roles described, is totally anonymous from any public point of view. The idea promoted here is that the anonymity offers in everyone's case a unique opportunity to stand back and resist the seductions of the media by seeing through them.

# Conclusion

We spoke of public space, or public spaces in the plural. Not streets, markets or pedestrian precincts, but an abstract space formed by a shared political landscape. Historically, the market-place does offer one example of a public space; the Athenian agora and the Roman forum were not just bounded physical spaces where people met, they were political arenas, places where at least male members of society could mingle with their representatives, senators, and other important political figures. But the ancient market-place has no true successors in the vastly expanded societies of today. The closest analogue is to be found in the corridors of power where the press, not the people, meet the powers that be, sometimes directly but more often through official briefings and carefully crafted communiqués.

Some people see in the expanding media a possibility of politically fruitful interaction between peoples and their representatives. The Internet is even presented as a worldwide electronic agora serving much the same functions as its ancient predecessor but on a global scale.

Another powerful line of thought sees it in another way. Rather than bridging the divide between outsider and insider, the media corrupt their discourse and drive a politically destructive wedge between them.[1]

That the media may assist in disseminating new visions and breaking down barriers caused by entrenched misunderstandings, traditional animosities and fear seems indisputable. The problem is rather with the public. Unlike the replicants, mentioned in the previous chapter, with their lack of place and history and unbound by the exigencies of locomotion, who would like what we possess, we, in our own constant verbal flights from our surroundings, seem intent on losing what we have. We vanish into talk shows, reality television, and the time spent doting on the web-sited preparations for the marriages of celebrities. By unresistingly grasping the now-vast opportunities offered by the media for voyeurism and illusions of intimacy with the great, we even appear to accept that we are nothing if not in the company of these 'true' human beings. What to the constant mobile-phoner is a conversation, and to those within earshot one half of a dialogue, is for the phoner an escape from the space we live in and share. It can be a life-saver in an emergency, but disembodied dialogues are not as a rule truly dialogues. They are mutant monologues designed to 'fill' time; they provide a way of speaking to yourself that relieves you of half the trouble of finding your own words. Here, and increasingly in public space in general, the silences that are part of normal conversation and integral to what is imparted aloud are impossible; the mobile-phoner's 'space' has to be constantly filled or else you have to keep on saying, 'Are you still there?'

Some will ask, 'Are they ever?' In such a location-ignoring, existence-draining form of communication the idea of 'where' loses all point. Some see in this the chance to establish wider communities not bound by distance and confined to like-minded souls, or to unite a global network sometimes characterized as 'spiritual' because disembodied. Others, in the more dust-raising spirit of a Voltaire, use the distance-destroying capacity of the Net to collect support for political engagement on the real globe. But as Kierkegaard more or less remarked, what kind of personal commitment is made by merely adding your name to a circular?[2] And while virtual communities along the information highway may seem to herald an exciting new future, it is hard not to see this search for new communities as due, in the words of a recent commentator, to a 'hunger for community' as 'more and more informal spaces disappear from real lives'.[3]

It is not unexpected that the image of the ancient marketplace has been invoked. 'The vision of a citizen-designed, citizen-controlled worldwide communications network', as the same writer says, 'is a version of technological utopianism that could be called the vision of "the electronic agora"'.[4] The analogy is quite persuasive. In this non-space we do 'meet' over vast distances to exchange gossip and views. Those over-eager to denigrate it with a 'brave new world' stamp might consider that the ancient agora and forum may also have been haunted by paedophiles and their like, and admit that in any case not all communication can be equally edifying. It would be hard for defenders of the Internet to deny, nonetheless, that the electronic agora offers a home to interests and activities of a kind that, if they existed at all in ancient times, belonged in other parts of town. Some might even say, metaphorically, that the electronic market has become the open sewer that in the ancient agora was channelled safely to the side, or the bawdy house whose clients would prefer a location less open to the public gaze.

As a vast reference library, the Internet does nevertheless allow us to gather and share information on an enormous variety of topics and with incredible speed. It forms a huge expansion of public space, less the public sphere as a place of testing debate than a public space or billboard on which messages can be hung and views pinned up for airing. It is an almost unlimited space in which the citizen can wander at will, diverting him- or herself with this and that, looking forever outwards at an infinite world of facts, at Wittgenstein's world of everything that is the case, though on the unedited billboard that is the Internet, there is the heavy task, so long as there is any interest in the distinction, of singling out fact from fiction.

One important thing lacking or liable to disappear is the sense of presence. There are many sides to this but two are worth noting. One is the illusion of having overcome distance. Does distance matter? Many assume not; they are impressed by how space can be overcome.[5] But surely it does matter, and space is not something we should gladly overcome except in order to secure co-presence; it is required for true openness. Not least there is the political aspect. The agora and forum owe their meaning historically more to this than to being just a combination of market and meeting place. As Dreyfus notes, compared with the kind of direct and open democracy made possible by being contained in those areas, the unbounded electronic agora is 'precisely the opposite of the public sphere'. Presenting views there is nothing like participation in a debate; one risks nothing and behaves more like a looker-on and busy-body with no personal engagement. In Dreyfus's view, 'As an extension to the deracinated public sphere, the electronic agora is a grave danger to real political community.'[6]

In fact, however, the electronic agora offers no footholds for communal life of any kind. The fledgling public sphere of the eighteenth-century coffee-house at least both talked community and in its small way was one. In this infinite non-space there is not even standing room. You may enter an Internet café and see people there. It is a space, but not a social space and certainly not a communal one. The customers are absenting themselves from each other in favour of relationships thinly re-invoked when catching up with their e-mail. The notion of space here empties itself. Not of what filled it but of space itself. To call it 'cyberspace', thereby implying that here we have not only another kind of space but one where communal life can be reconstructed as global inter-communication, is to invoke a myth that the reflective individual, sufficiently outside, should have little difficulty in exploding.

But beyond this, presence is also a condition of genuine perception, both of what stands before you and of your own relationship to that. The ability to work out the world from where you stand is a pre-condition of learning to know yourself in your perceptions of it. Breaking the circle in which the media serve a politically passive public, so as to generate a public debate that is critical and open, requires an ability on the side of the public to see, and draw attention to, the failures of judgement and openness among those who decide public affairs, as much as it requires open and critical debate on the part of the public.

Habermas has stressed the need of the latter. But what is this but a proposal to revert to the situation of the public's origins in a view like Dewey's in which the public is a self-originating and self-helping organizer of its own governmental arrangements? It is as if to say that the way the public came into being is also the way it should be preserved and constantly renewed. It implies or requires that Lippmann's outsider/insider distinction can be overcome. But it cannot.

Consequently, what is needed is not a proliferation of grass-root debate among an outsider electorate but pressure exerted on insiders to make their own policy-making discussions or debates open and critical. Such pressure can only come from outside. Certainly it will not issue from those commercial interests that constrain even the insiders. It may need new Voltaires.

To a politically awakening public the injustices Voltaire brought to its notice were glaring. The truths a contemporary must try to place in the public mind are harder to see and sometimes as hard to accept. But if the furore Voltaire could arouse cannot be repeated so easily today, that is not because there are no Voltaires; the press is well staffed with excellent writers who are perceptive critics of the political scene. It is because, as Lippmann pointed out, the public's mind is elsewhere: efforts to enlighten it are like trying to make water stick to a duck's back. But if the public will not be enlightened by the media, then it must be enlightened by itself, which means by those among it still able to find the time and space to look for themselves, in both senses, and to hearken to the voices of new Voltaires.

## ONE   THE PUBLIC

1 John Tusa (ex-journalist), 'Don't attack the BBC – you can't win', *Guardian*, 22 July 2003.

2 John Dewey remarks on the significance of 'private' being defined in opposition to 'official' (see Chapter 5 below), but in the sense of 'one deprived of public position' (John Dewey, *The Public and its Problems*, Athens, Ohio: Swallow Press/Ohio University Press, 1954, p. 15).

3 *Plutarch's Lives*, Dryden's edn, rev. with intro. by Arthur Hugh Clough, Everyman's Library, London: J. M. Dent & Sons/New York: E. P. Dutton & Co., 1910, Vol. II, pp. 277–8.

4 Cicero, *De re publica/De legibus*, Vol. XVI of *Cicero in Twenty-Eight Volumes*, trans. Clinton Walker Keyes, London: Heinemann/Cambridge, Mass.: Harvard University Press, pp. 221–2.

5 William Shakespeare, *Julius Caesar*, Act III, Scene 2.

6 Cf. the case of one citizen, St Paul (Acts 22: 22–9). I owe this reference to an anonymous reader.

7 Dewey, op. cit., p. 35.

8 Ibid., p. 67.

9 Ibid., pp. 15–16.

10 Ibid., p. 113.

11 Ibid., p. 137.

12 Ibid., p. 137.

## TWO   PUBLIC AS AUDIENCE

1 Arthur Herman, *How the Scots Invented the Modern World: the true story of how western Europe's poorest nation created our world and everything in it*, New York: Three Rivers Press, 2001, p. 184.

2 F. H. Allport some time ago (*Institutional Behavior* (87), 1933) wrote: 'Since the public is no specific group of individuals, but is defined wholly by the range of the common interest in a particular transaction, there may be a separate public for every issue raised.' He concludes: 'We are compelled, therefore, to think of many publics.' Dewey's discussion is devoted to showing how a state can have its public, referring on the way to various 'forms of union' not yet amounting to states and to what they lack to become states. He also talks of states that lack publics, and of what would be needed to acquire them.

3 An anonymous reader of a previous draft suggested bands with cult followings as an example. This interesting suggestion raises further questions, in particular whether followings really deserve to be called publics, and whether whatever scruples we have against calling them that are mirrored in a similar reluctance to describe a church congregation as a public.

## THREE  THE PUBLIC SPHERE

1 Jürgen Habermas, *The Structural Transformation of the Public Sphere: an inquiry into a category of bourgeois society*, trans. Thomas Burger with the assistance of Frederick Lawrence, Oxford: Polity Press, 1989, p. 31.

2 Ibid., p. 85.

3 See James Gleick, *Isaac Newton*, New York: Pantheon Books, 2003.

4 So called by the Whigs, for being bloodless, but it is thought also because their programme of constitutional reform proved to benefit by it.

5 As to whether literature itself could then be regarded as an effective instrument of social reform, there is a hint of a reservation in the remark of that paradigmatic Augustan, Alexander Pope. He said that if only he, Dean Swift and the Tory writer and politician Viscount Bolingbroke were able to live and write together for three years, the combined effect of their satiric output could 'accomplish some good even upon this age' (see Alexander Witherspoon [gen. ed.], *College Survey of English Literature*, rev. shorter edn, New York: Harcourt, Brace & Co., 1951, p. 487). The remark should be considered in light of the fact that the 'age' was one in which these writers saw menace in Robert Walpole's Whiggish ambitions for a more powerful parliament.

6 Frederick C. Beiser, *Enlightenment, Revolution, and Romanticism: the genesis of*

*modern German political thought 1790–1800*, Cambridge, Mass.: Harvard University Press, 1992, p. 50.

7 Ibid., p. 51.

8 Ibid., p. 53.

9 Ibid., pp. 53 and 374 n. 113.

10 Walter Lippmann, *The Phantom Public*, New Brunswick, NJ/London: Transaction Publishers [1927], 2003, p. 67.

11 Søren Kierkegaard, *A Literary Review*, trans. Alastair Hannay, Harmondsworth: Penguin, 2001, pp. 81–2.

12 Lippmann, op. cit., p. 3.

13 Ibid., pp. 28–9.

14 Cf. ibid., p. 12.

15 Ibid., p. 140.

16 Thomas McCarthy, 'Habermas', in S. Critchley and W. R. Schroeder (eds), *A Companion to Continental Philosophy*, Oxford: Blackwell, 1998, p. 404.

## FOUR   PUBLIC OPINION

1 Lippmann, op. cit., pp. 56–7 and 64.

2 Charles Taylor, *Social Imaginaries*, Durham, NC/London: Duke University Press, 2002, p. 6.

3 David Hume, *Hume's Moral and Political Philosophy*, ed. with intro. by Henry D. Aiken, New York: Hafner Publishing Co., 1959, p. 374.

4 See Herman, op. cit., pp. 259–60.

5 Hume, op. cit., pp. 384–5.

6 Ibid., p. 375.

7 Ibid., p. 385.

8 Dewey, op. cit., p. 115.

9 Hume, op. cit., p. 384.

10 Ibid., p. 371.

11 John Ralston Saul, *Voltaire's Bastards: the dictatorship of reason in the west*, New York: Vintage Books, 1993, p. 320.

12 See Gustave Lanson's biography, *Voltaire*, Paris: Hachette, 1960, pp. 193ff.

13 Saul, op. cit., p. 320.

14 Ibid., pp. 320–1.

15 Lanson (op. cit., p. 191) says that Voltaire was without doubt a *conservateur*, but in a way that was altogether 'liberal'.

16 Gertrude Himmelfarb, 'The Idea of Compassion: the British vs. the French Enlightenment', *The Public Interest* (Fall 2001).

17 Hume, op. cit., p. 374.

18 Richard Sennett, *Authority*, New York: Vintage Books, 1981, p. 188.

19 Hume cites the seventeenth-century French prelate, Cardinal de Retz, who proclaimed that 'all numerous assemblies, however composed, are mere mob, and swayed in their debates by the least motive', something Hume takes to be 'confirmed by daily experience': 'When an absurdity strikes a member, he conveys it to his neighbour, and so on till the whole be infected' (op. cit., p. 380).

20 Ibid., p. 380.

## FIVE   EMPTYING PUBLIC SPACE

1 Dewey, op. cit., p. 15.

2 Samuel Warren and Louis D. Brandeis, 'The Right to Privacy', 4 *Harvard Law Review* 193 (1890), first page. See Patricia Meyer Spacks, *Privacy: concealing the eighteenth-century self*, Chicago, Ill.: University of Chicago Press, 2003. The passage is sometimes rendered incorrectly as 'the right to be left alone', which has a more anti-social feel.

3 See G. W. F. Hegel, *Schriften zur Politik und Rechtsphilosophie*, ed. G. Lasson, Leipzig: Meiner, 1923, p. 140.

4 'Aphorisms from the Wastebook', in Jon Stewart (ed.), *Miscellaneous Writings of G. W. F. Hegel*, Evanston, Ill.: Northwestern University Press, 2002, p. 247. (Cf. Shlomo Avineri, *Hegel's Theory of the Modern State*, Cambridge: Cambridge University Press, 1972, p. 38).

5 Hannah Arendt, *The Human Condition*, Chicago, Ill.: Chicago University Press, 1958, p. 58.

6 See Howard Rheingold's balanced discussion of such claims in his *The Virtual Community: homesteading on the electronic frontier*, New York: HarperCollins/Perennial, 1994, rev. edn, Cambridge, Mass.: MIT Press, 2000.

7 Johannes Hoffmeister (ed.), *Dokumente zu Hegels Entwicklung*, Stuttgart: Fromann, 1936, p. 358.

8 *Hegel's Philosophy of Right*, trans. T. M. Knox, Oxford: Oxford University Press, 1952, pp. 161 and 168. Marital love, involving permission, ties and 'free surrender of personality . . . by both sexes' was love that had become aware of itself.

## SIX  PRIVACY AND THE MEDIA

1  Each of these two potentially critical factors has been a topic of a long tradition of social psychology, the former traceable to the Danish writer Søren Kierkegaard and the latter to Hegel, the thinker Kierkegaard is most famed for criticizing They are topics concerning social life in general, and although they do relate to our own topic, what we are specifically considering here are the effects of a public space monopolized by the media.

2  Richard Sennett, *The Fall of Public Man: on the social psychology of capitalism*, New York: Vintage Books, 1978, pp. 287ff.

3  For an informed comment, see Howard Rheingold, *Smart Mobs: the next social revolution*, Cambridge, Mass.: Perseus Publishing, 2002, p. 121.

## SEVEN  A COMMON SENSE

1  Hume, op. cit., p. 371.

2  See Chapter 4, p. 53.

3  Lippmann, op. cit., p. 55.

4  See Samantha Power, *A Problem from Hell: America and the age of genocide*, New York: HarperCollins/Perennial, 2003.

5  Closer, in spirit, is John Rawls's notion of a 'reflective equilibrium', a state in which principles based on initial intuitions have been successively replaced by others that accord with a greater number of intuitions, to bring about a harmony between intuitions, now better called considered judgements, and principles. See John Rawls, *A Theory of Justice*, Cambridge, Mass.: Harvard University Press, 1971.

6  Peter Singer, 'Bioethics and academic freedom', *Bioethics* (4) 1990, p. 33. See my 'What Can Philosophers Contribute to Social Ethics?', *Topoi* 17 (2) 1998, pp. 127–36, from which this discussion is partly extracted, by kind permission of Kluwer Academic Publishers © 1998 Kluwer Academic Publishers.

7  Singer, op. cit., pp. 43 and 44.

8  See Julia A. Moore, 'More than a Food Fight', in *Issues in Science and Technology* (Summer, 2001).

9  Thucydides, *Thucydides' Peloponnesian War*, trans. Richard Crawley, London: Dent, 1903, Vol. I, p. 141.

### EIGHT  TRANSFORMING THE PRIVATE SPHERE

1   See Victor Turner, *Dramas, Fields, and Metaphors: symbolic action in human society*, Ithaca, NY/London: Cornell University Press, 1974, esp. Chapter 5.

2   See Jürgen Habermas, *The Theory of Communicative Action*, Vol. II: *Lifeworld and System: a critique of functionalist reason*, trans. T. McCarthy, Boston, Mass.: Beacon Press, 1987.

3   Jürgen Habermas, *The Philosophical Discourse of Modernity*, trans. F. Lawrence, Oxford: Polity Press, 1987, p. 96.

4   Hubert L. Dreyfus, *On the Internet*, London and New York: Routledge, 2001, p. 76.

5   Ibid., p. 75.

### CONCLUSION

1   See notably Leon H. Mayhew, *The New Public: professional communication and the means of social influence*, Cambridge: Cambridge University Press, 1997.

2   See Søren Kierkegaard, *Concluding Unscientific Postscript*, trans. Howard V. Hong and Edna H. Hong, Princeton, NJ: Princeton University Press, 1992, p. 243 (in the Swenson and Lowrie trans., Princeton, NJ: Princeton University Press, 1941, p. 217). *Søren Kierkegaards Skrifter* (SKS), ed. N. J. Cappelørn, J. Garff, J. Kondrup, A. McKinnon and F. H. Mortensen, Copenhagen: Gads Forlag, 1997–, SKS 7, 2002, p. 221.

3   Rheingold, op. cit., p. 6.

4   Ibid., p. 14. Quoted (from revised edn, Cambridge, Mass.: MIT Press, 2000) and discussed by Dreyfus, op. cit., pp. 103ff.

5   See Rheingold, *Smart Mobs*, op. cit., Chapter 7, 'Smart Mobs: the power of the mobile many'.

6   Dreyfus, op. cit., p. 104.

# Bibliography

Allport, F. H., *Institutional Behavior*, vol. 87, 1933.

Arendt, Hannah, *The Human Condition*, Chicago, Ill.: Chicago University Press, 1958.

Avineri, Shlomo, *Hegel's Theory of the Modern State*, Cambridge: Cambridge University Press, 1972.

Baudrillard, Jean, *America*, trans. Chris Turner, London: Verso Books, 1986.

Beiser, Frederick C., *Enlightenment, Revolution, and Romanticism: the genesis of modern German political thought 1790–1800*, Cambridge, Mass.: Harvard University Press, 1992.

Castells, Manuel, *Internet Galaxy*, New York: Oxford University Press, 2001.

Cicero (Marcus Tullius Cicero), *De re publica/De legibus*, Vol. XVI of *Cicero in Twenty-Eight Volumes*, trans. Clinton Walker Keyes, London: Heinemann/ Cambridge, Mass.: Harvard University Press.

Critchley, S. and W. R. Schroeder (eds), *A Companion to Continental Philosophy*, Oxford: Blackwell, 1998.

Dewey, John, *The Public and its Problems*, Athens, Ohio: Ohio University Press, 1954.

Dreyfus, Hubert L., *On the Internet*, London and New York: Routledge, 2001.

Fowler, Alastair, 'Frolics with the Oyster Wenches' (review of Mary Cosh, *Edinburgh: The Golden Age*, Edinburgh: John Donald, 2003), *TLS*, 6 June 2003, p. 10.

Gleick, James, *Isaac Newton*, New York: Pantheon Books, 2003.

Habermas, Jürgen, *The Philosophical Discourse of Modernity*, trans. Frederick Lawrence, Oxford: Polity Press, 1987.

—— *The Theory of Communicative Action*, Vol II: *Lifeworld and System: a critique of functionalist reason*, trans. Thomas McCarthy, Boston, Mass.: Beacon Press, 1987.

—— *The Structural Transformation of the Public Sphere: an inquiry into a category of bourgeois society*, trans. Thomas Burger with the assistance of Frederick Lawrence, Oxford: Polity Press, 1989.

Hannay, Alastair, 'What Can Philosophers Contribute to Social Ethics?', *Topoi* 17(2) 1998, pp. 127–36.

Hegel, G. W. F., *Schriften zur Politik und Rechtsphilosophie*, ed. G. Lasson, Leipzig: Meiner, 1923.

—— *Hegel's Philosophy of Right*, trans. T. M. Knox, Oxford: Oxford University Press, 1952.

Herman, Arthur, *How the Scots Invented the Modern World: the true story of how western Europe's poorest nation created our world and everything in it*, New York: Three Rivers Press, 2001.

Himmelfarb, Gertrude, 'The Idea of Compassion: the British vs. the French Enlightenment', *The Public Interest* (Fall) 2001.

Hoffmeister, Johannes (ed.), *Dokumente zu Hegels Entwicklung*, Stuttgart: Fromann, 1936.

Hume, David, *Hume's Moral and Political Philosophy*, ed. with intro. by Henry D. Aiken, New York: Hafner Publishing Co., 1959.

Kierkegaard, Søren, *Søren Kierkegaards Papirer*, 2nd edn, N. Thulstrup, Copenhagen: Gyldendal, 1968.

—— *Concluding Unscientific Postscript*, trans. Howard V. Hong and Edna H. Hong, Princeton, NJ: Princeton University Press, 1992.

—— *Either/Or: a fragment of life*, trans. Alastair Hannay, Harmondsworth: Penguin, 1992.

—— *A Literary Review*, trans. Alastair Hannay, Harmondsworth: Penguin, 2001.

Lanson, Gustave, *Voltaire*, Paris: Hachette, 1960.

Lyon, David, *Postmodernity*, Milton Keynes: Open University Press, 1994.

McCarthy, Thomas, 'Habermas', in S. Critchley and W. R. Schroeder (eds), *A Companion to Continental Philosophy*, Oxford: Blackwell, 1998.

McCaughey, Mary and Michael D. Ayers (eds), *Cyberactivism: online activism in theory and practice*, London and New York: Routledge, 2003.

Mayhew, Leon H., *The New Public: professional communication and the means of social influence*, Cambridge: Cambridge University Press, 1997.

Melucci, Alberto, *Nomads of the Present: social movements and individual needs in contemporary society*, Philadelphia, Pa.: Temple University Press, 1989.

Moore, Julia A., 'More than a Food Fight', *Issues in Science and Technology* (Summer) 2001.

Nesse, Åse-Marie, 'En salong i Berlin: Rahel Varnhagen', in Kari Vogt *et al.*, *Kvinnenes kulturhistorie*, 2, Oslo: Universitetsforlaget, 1985, pp. 22–4.

Plutarch, *Plutarch's Lives*, Dryden's edn, rev. with intro. by Arthur Hugh Clough, London: J. M. Dent & Sons/New York: E. P. Dutton & Co., 1910, Vol. II.

Popper, Karl R., *The Open Society and its Enemies*, 2 volumes, London: Routledge & Kegan Paul, 1945.

Power, Samantha, *A Problem from Hell: America and the age of genocide*, New York: HarperCollins/Perennial, 2003.

Rawls, John, *A Theory of Justice*, Cambridge, Mass.: Harvard University Press, 1971.

Rheingold, Howard, *The Virtual Community: homesteading on the electronic frontier*, New York: HarperCollins/Perennial, 1994; rev. edn, Cambridge, Mass.: MIT Press, 2000.

—— *Smart Mobs: the next social revolution*, Cambridge, Mass.: Perseus Publishing, 2002.

Saul, John Ralston, *Voltaire's Bastards: the dictatorship of reason in the west*, New York: Vintage Books, 1993.

Schudson, Michael, *Watergate in American Memory: how we remember, forget, and reconstruct the past*, New York: Basic Books, 1992.

—— *The Good Citizen: a history of American civic life*, Cambridge, Mass.: Harvard University Press, 1999.

Sennett, Richard, *The Fall of Public Man: on the social psychology of capitalism*, New York: Vintage Books, 1978 (New York: Alfred A. Knopf, 1977).

—— *Authority*, New York: Vintage Books, 1981 (New York: Alfred A. Knopf, 1980).

Singer, Peter, 'Bioethics and academic freedom', *Bioethics* (4), 1990, 33–44.

Spacks, Patricia Meyer, *Privacy: concealing the eighteenth-century self*, Chicago, Ill.: University of Chicago Press, 2003.

Stewart, Jon (ed.), *Miscellaneous Writings of G.W.F. Hegel*, Evanston, Ill.: Northwestern University Press, 2002.

Taylor, Charles, *Modern Social Imaginaries*, Public Planet Books, Durham, NC and London: Duke University Press, 2004.

Thucydides, *Thucydides' Peloponnesian War*, trans. Richard Crawley, London: J. M. Dent & Sons, 1904, Vol. I.

Turner, Victor, *Dramas, Fields, and Metaphors: symbolic action in human society*, Ithaca, NY: Cornell University Press, 1974.

Turkle, Sherry, *Life on the Screen: identity in the age of the Internet*, New York: Simon & Schuster, 1995.

Varnhagen, Rahel, *Briefe und Aufzeichnungen*, Frankfurt: Insel Verlag, 1986.

Warren, Samuel and Louis D. Brandeis, 'The Right to Privacy', 4 *Harvard Law Review* (193) 1890.

Witherspoon, Alexander (gen. ed.), *College Survey of English Literature*, rev. shorter edn, New York: Harcourt, Brace & Company, 1951.